The Stonewall Brigade: The History ̣ ̣̣ ̣ ̣ ̣ ̣̣ ̣ ̣Most Famous Confederate Combat Unit of the Civil War

By Charles River Editors

A portrait of Stonewall Jackson

About Charles River Editors

Charles River Editors provides superior editing and original writing services across the digital publishing industry, with the expertise to create digital content for publishers across a vast range of subject matter. In addition to providing original digital content for third party publishers, we also republish civilization's greatest literary works, bringing them to new generations of readers via ebooks.

Sign up here to receive updates about free books as we publish them, and visit Our Kindle Author Page to browse today's free promotions and our most recently published Kindle titles.

Introduction

Stonewall Jackson

The Stonewall Brigade

"There is Jackson standing like a stone wall. Let us determine to die here, and we will conquer. Rally behind the Virginians." – General Barnard Bee

April 18, 1861 marked the date Southern forces started pouring into Harper's Ferry, Virginia. Six days earlier, shots had been fired at Fort Sumter in Charleston Harbor, South Carolina, marking the beginning of the Civil War, and Virginia officially seceded from the Union April 17. The following day, men arrived in the town where John Brown's attempted uprising was quelled less than two years earlier. The men came from all portions of the Confederate States of America (C.S.A.) and the border states of Kentucky and Maryland, but the preponderance of volunteers came from Virginia.

Once the Confederate troops occupied Harpers Ferry, martial law was declared and so-called "feather bed" Confederate military officers, often referred to as "swells," were replaced by professional soldiers with military training. One such man who arrived from the Virginia Military Institute (VMI) was Thomas Jonathan Jackson, who on April 27 was ordered by Virginia Governor John Letcher to take control of the troops converging on Harpers Ferry. He did as ordered and began to form what became the renowned Stonewall Brigade.

Jackson and his brigade earned the nickname "Stonewall" at First Manassas by turning the tide of that battle, and they would become known as the legendary foot cavalry by bottling up 3 different Union armies in the Shenandoah Valley in 1862. Although Stonewall Jackson and the Stonewall Brigade may share the most famous nickname to come out of the Civil War, it's still unclear whether Barnard Bee, the general who provided the legendary name at First Manassas, meant it as a complaint that they were not moving or as a compliment for standing resolute in the heat of battle.

Regardless, the Stonewall Brigade went on to fight in every major battle in the Eastern theater of the American Civil War, to the extent that of the 6,000 men who fought with the brigade over the course of four years, less than 200 remained by the time General Robert E. Lee surrendered at Appomattox Courthouse on April 9, 1865. They were organized, trained, and mentored by one of the most revered military leaders in American history, and they made a decisive impact on battles like First Manassas, the 1862 Valley Campaign, and Chancellorsville. The brigade was virtually a spent force by the end of the Battle of Spotsylvania Courthouse in May 1864, which took place nearly a year after Stonewall Jackson himself had been mortally wounded at Chancellorsville.

Not only was the Stonewall Brigade present at most of the major engagements in the Eastern theater, more often than not, they were positioned at the edge of the front line of battle. It can be fairly stated that while these men may not have been more heroic or courageous than any other soldiers who fought in the Civil War, they appeared in the first wave of volunteers immediately after Virginia announced secession, were better trained, were more skillfully directed, and showed greater dedication to the cause and their leader than most regiments on either side of the conflict. Stonewall Jackson trusted and relied upon his soldiers of the 1st Brigade, Virginia Volunteers, to a far greater degree than other generals relied on their subordinates, with one possible exception; General Robert E. Lee's reliance on Stonewall Jackson himself. Of course, the brigade itself played a crucial role in making Jackson Lee's "right arm."

The Stonewall Brigade: The History of the Most Famous Confederate Combat Unit of the Civil War looks at one of the Civil War's most legendary brigades. Along with pictures of important people, places, and events, you will learn about the Stonewall Brigade like never before.

The Stonewall Brigade: The History of the Most Famous Confederate Combat Unit of the Civil War

About Charles River Editors

Introduction

Chapter 1: Stonewall Jackson and the Organization of the Brigade

Five days after the attack on Fort Sumter, Virginia seceded from the U.S. Harper's Ferry, Virginia was not only an important strategic point in the War, as it sat on the mouth of the Potomac River and at the bottom of the plush Shenandoah Valley, it was also a major armory. Seizing this town meant a supply route and an arsenal of weapons for the Confederacy. Not only was there a cache of arms available but also the equipment and means by which to produce more weapons.[1] With the fertile Shenandoah Valley to feed them, the Potomac River to protect them, and the machinery to arm them, Harper's Ferry was the ideal place to amass and train troops.

One of the principal commanders who would train the soldiers at Harper's Ferry was Thomas Jonathan Jackson. Born on January 21, 1824 in Clarksburg, Virginia (now West Virginia), Jackson had a turbulent childhood. His father died when he was only three years of age, prompting his mother, Julia, to send Thomas and his brother to live with their uncle. Frequently unsatisfied with his living arrangements, he and his cousins often fled their home and sought accommodations with other relatives. Inevitably, Jackson returned to his uncle's home and when schoolrooms were available, he had to work extremely hard at his studies in order to keep pace with his classmates.[2]

Jackson tried his hand at different professions after completing his preliminary education. When he heard news of an unexpected cadet vacancy at West Point Military Academy, he was excited at the prospect of furthering his education in an area that was of great interest to him. Due to his prior academic performance, he was forced to beg favors and prove he was capable of maintaining a satisfactory execution of duties and scholarship. He did just that and reported as a cadet in June 1842.

West Point held the same intellectual challenges for Jackson as had his previous schooling; however, he was not one to fail and pushed himself to far greater lengths than were necessary for his peers. A former classmate stated that "'He had a rough time in the Academy at first, for his want of previous training placed him at a great disadvantage, and it was all he could do to pass his first examination.'" The friend also remembered that "'all light were put out at 'taps,' and just before the signal he would pile up his grate with anthracite coal, and, lying prone before it on the floor, would work away at his lessons by the glare of the fire.'" His class mate remembered his group of friends saying, "'If we had to stay here another year, 'old Jack' would be at the head of the class.'"[3] This speaks to Jackson's dedication, not only to learning, but to excelling in whatever task he undertook. His diligence was rewarded when he graduated as 2nd Lieutenant of

---

[1] Thomas Cutrer. Lecture (Arizona State University, Glendale, Arizona, March 2, 2011).

[2] Mary Anna Jackson, *Memoirs of "Stonewall" Jackson* (Louisville, Prentice Press, 1895), 11-25. Mrs. Jackson writes an excellent account of her husband's life. Although she is biased at times, the memoir contains countless letters from Jackson and first-hand accounts from herself and witnesses of historical events. This is recommended reading for anyone interested in the personal aspects of Jackson's life and offers an insight into his psychological make-up.

[3] Jackson, 33.

artillery on June 30, 1846.

As he and his classmates (including George McClellan and George Pickett among others) were graduating, the Mexican-American War was underway, and he was immediately deployed with his class to Mexico. On March 9, 1847, as a member of the 1st Regiment of Artillery, Jackson landed on the beach at Vera Cruz. As a reward for his gallantry in action during this battle, he was promoted to captain. Another promotion was forthcoming after his heroics in maintaining his position during the storming of Chapultepec.

When the war concluded, Major Thomas J. Jackson was first stationed at Fort Hamilton on Long Island, New York for two years followed by a six month stint at Fort Meade in Florida. Unhappy with these posts, Jackson was exuberant when he was reassigned as an instructor at the Virginia Military Institute (VMI) in Lexington. On March 27, 1851 he assumed the position of Professor of Natural and Experimental Philosophy and Artillery Tactics.[4]

Jackson's life continued to see happiness as he married his first wife, Elinor in August 1853. Tragedy struck; however, 14 months hence as Elinor died while giving birth to their still born daughter. After much suffering and grief, in 1857 he wed for a second time to Mary Anna.

In the autumn of 1859, as he was enjoying his domestic life and work at VMI, he was ordered to take his troops to Harper's Ferry for the execution of John Brown. There was concern on the part of the government that a second uprising might occur in the shadows of Brown's hanging and troops were needed to put down any such insurrection. No unrest took place that day, December 2, 1859, other than the execution of the controversial abolitionist. In a letter written to his wife on the day of the hanging, Jackson described the procedure of the execution as being "well-made." He also noted that once Brown was dead, "There was very little motion of his person for several moments, and soon the wind blew his lifeless body to and fro."[5]

After the execution John Brown, Jackson returned to VMI with his cadets. Although daily activities seemed to resume as before, the notoriety of John Brown and the subsequent election of Abraham Lincoln the following year brought war closer to Virginia. Mary Anna Jackson claims that her husband was never in favor of secession but that he felt it his duty to defend his home and that of his ancestors. Like so many, he felt that his primary obligation was to Virginia. He had hoped for a political resolution, hoping to avoid war, having witnessed the atrocities of war in Mexico, and he believed both sides took the notion of war too lightly. He confided in his pastor that he had seen enough of war to look upon it as the "sum of all evils," and was aware of the safety from which the advocates of war spoke, claiming, "They do not know its horrors."[6]

Nonetheless, Jackson was about to be thrust into war for a second time where he was destined

---

[4] Jackson, 53.
[5] Jackson, 130-131.
[6] Jackson, 141.

to lead fellow Virginians onto the battlefields of the Civil War. Though Jackson fundamentally opposed secession from the Union, upon the outbreak of the Civil War, he went with his native state of Virginia when it seeded, offering his services to the Confederacy. Jackson even brought some of the cadets he was training at VMI.

Almost immediately following Virginia's order to secede, Virginia Governor John Letcher ordered the seizure of Harper's Ferry. Local militias took action and a great number of volunteers from the Shenandoah Valley descended upon the town. Jackson was promoted to Colonel and given the arduous assignment of organizing and training these men.

It must be understood the manner in which an army is organized. The smallest unit of organization is a Company, comprised of 100 men from the same town under the command of a captain. A Regiment is formed by combining ten companies and placing them under the command of a colonel. While companies are designated by letters (A-K), regiments are called by numbers. Next is termed a Brigade which is composed of anywhere from two to five regiments and placed under the direction of a Brigadier General. The next largest is the Division, commanded by a Major General and consisting of two or more brigades. Following that is a Corps, led by a three star general and containing two or more divisions. Finally, there is an Army which consists of two or more corps and is under the ultimate command of a four star general.[7] It is therefore not an overstatement to say that Jackson's diligence and commitment were to be tested to the utmost.

---

[7] Cutrer, Lecture, March 2, 2011.

Letcher

The men coming into Harpers Ferry were volunteers with no military background. The came with the companies formed in their local towns and communities wearing a plethora of different colored uniforms, if any at all. Many arrived in their own clothing without as much as a gun. They were armed with what was available and slowly organized into regiments and finally brigades. The 1st Brigade, Virginia Volunteers was formally organized on April 27, 1861 and was composed of 2nd, 4th, 5th, and 27th Virginia Regiments (one month later to be joined by the 33rd), along with the Rockbridge Artillery Battery.[8] In a letter dated June 4, 1861, Jackson wrote to his wife, "The troops here have been divided into brigades, and the Virginia forces under General Johnston constitute the First Brigade, of which I am in command."[9] Five short weeks after writing this letter, the 1st Virginia would forever after be known as the Stonewall Brigade.

The men of this brigade were much like Jackson himself. Whereas a great deal of the

---

[8] Steven M. Smith and Patrick Hook, *The Stonewall Brigade in the Civil War* (Minneapolis: Zenith Press, 2008), 10-11.
[9] Jackson, 159.

high ranking West Point graduates who commanded the Southern forces were of the "gentleman" class and upbringing, Thomas Jackson was reared in the rocky hills of western Virginia. Prior to being admitted to West Point, he came from a fatherless home and was raised by relatives other than his widowed mother. He was a hard working physical man who held no truck with idleness or fainthearted actions. Many of the troops under his command came from similar backgrounds, sans the West Point education. Laborers, farmers, and mill workers who lacked any formal education and social graces made-up most of the 1st Brigade and were thereby relatable to their commander.

When the call to arms went out to Virginians, they responded mightily. One young man received information that a company had been raised in his native town of Springfield. He discovered they were in service a mere fifteen miles away and he "bade farewell to my parents and sisters and went to the company."[10] Once he arrived at camp, he "met old schoolmates…whom I had parted from two years before in the school room, and now found them in arms." He then signed the muster sheet, "put on the uniform of the gray, and was mustered into service for one year."[11] The same actions were repeated by thousands of Virginia men, both young and old, who were destined for the brutality of war. In order to best prepare such men, Jackson was relentless in the drilling of his troops.

Shortly after being promoted to Brigadier General and assuming command of the 1st Brigade, a newspaper made mention of Jackson and the aptitude he possessed. The media outlet noted, "'Born in Virginia, educated at West Point, trained in the Mexican war, occupied since at the pet military institution of the Old Dominion, his whole life has been a preparation for this struggle.'"[12] He was, in fact well prepared and in short order made sure the same was true of his volunteers.

The roughly 2,500 men of the 1st Brigade, initially part of the Virginia Provisional Army, were assigned to Joseph Johnston's Army of the Shenandoah (consisting of approximately 11,000 troops) on May 15, 1861. One month hence, General J. Johnson realized that Harpers Ferry had become untenable and was forced to evacuate, but not before destroying the armaments and machinery the town held. He and Jackson led their troops close to Winchester, engaging in few small battles and skirmishes along the way. The first significant test of battle, for both sides, was looming closer as the armies would meet in July in Manassas, Virginia.

---

[10] John O. Casler, *Four Years in the Stonewall Brigade*, 2nd ed., 1906 (Endeavour Press, 2016), location 137, Kindle. This is a riveting and honest account of a Confederate Private. Many low-ranked Southern soldiers was unable to read due to the unavailability of education thereby making the number of memoirs and journals from such men limited. Northern soldiers, in general, had a higher level of education and produced a greater number of accurate and well-written works.

[11] Casler, location 137.

[12] Jackson, 156.

Johnston

As the summer of 1861 wore on, General Johnston's army remained quartered near Winchester while Beauregard's larger army was positioned around Manassas, Virginia. This spot held a key railroad junction that was coveted by the Confederate Army. Troop transport via train was first used in the U.S. during the Civil War and the depot in Manassas was of strategic importance as it was only 20 miles from Washington, D.C. The Confederacy needed to fend off the invading Yankees, as they were called, in order to maintain a rail supply route. Additionally, if the Union troops took possession of Manassas Junction and captured Beauregard's 21,000 men, a relatively easy path to Richmond was available.

Private John O. Casler was a member of the Potomac Guards, A-company, 33rd Virginia infantry regiment. The 33rd was part of the 1st Brigade, Virginia Volunteers until July 15, 1861. Casler remembered being marched from his position "one mile north to Winchester and permanently attached to T.J. Jackson's Brigade."[13] The 33rd was not yet numbered and were simply referred to as Colonel Cummings' Regiment. Private Casler and his comrades arrived at Bull Run creek on July 20. That night the troops rested on their arms and discussed the inevitable battle that was about to commence. Casler and his messmate, William I. Blue discussed "the realities of war in its most horrible form   brother against brother, father against son, kindred against kindred, and our country torn to pieces by civil war." That night Casler and Blue pledged to one another that if one man was killed during battle, the survivor was to see that the other was buried.[14]

---

[13] Casler, location 205.
[14] Casler, location 223-229.

Chapter 2: There Stands Jackson Like a Stone Wall

As Johnston went about gathering and training additional troops in the Shenandoah Valley, Jefferson Davis ordered the hero of Fort Sumter, P.G.T. Beauregard, to northern Virginia as second-in-command to Johnston, where he was to oppose the Union forces building up near Washington under the command of Irvin McDowell. Though Johnston was the superior in rank, he ceded authority to Beauregard near Manassas Junction, which was about 60 miles away from the Shenandoah Valley, leaving Beauregard in command there. Beauregard took charge of the Confederate forces assembling near the rail junction at Manassas and had his men construct defenses along a 14 mile front along Bull Run Creek.

As the Confederates were preparing, a Union army called the Army of Northeastern Virginia (not to be confused with Lee's legendary Army of Northern Virginia) was being assembled under the command of 42 year old Irvin McDowell, who was promoted to brigadier general in the regular army on May 14, 1861, despite the fact he had never commanded soldiers in battle. McDowell got the spot as a result of politics, thanks to the influence of his friend and mentor Salmon Chase, Lincoln's Treasury Secretary. Although McDowell was inexperienced, he was savvy enough to know that the politicians around Washington spurring him to action were overeager and operating under the belief that there might be one climactic battle before the Union army marched to Richmond and put down the rebellion in its cradle. But McDowell's reluctance and protests that his men were too raw and not ready were countered by President Lincoln, who pointed out, "You are green, it is true, but they are green also; you are all green alike."

While Lincoln's point was true, it naively discounted the advantage of defensive warfare over offensive warfare during the Civil War era. Civil War generals began the war employing tactics from the Napoleonic Era, which saw Napoleon dominate the European continent and win crushing victories against large armies. However, the weapons available in 1861 were far more accurate than they had been 50 years earlier. In particular, new rifled barrels created common infantry weapons with deadly accuracy of up to 100 yards, at a time when generals were still leading massed infantry charges with fixed bayonets and attempting to march their men close enough to engage in hand-to-hand combat.

McDowell

As a result of the political pressure, McDowell was forced to start his offensive in the summer of 1861 against the Confederates in his front in Northern Virginia. Thus, on July 16, McDowell moved forward at the head of a nearly 35,000 man army, the largest ever assembled in North America, striking out west in three columns. McDowell knew that he outnumbered Beauregard's men at Manassas, and he was counting on an 18,000 man army led by General Robert Patterson to menace Johnston's 10,000 strong Army of the Shenandoah in the Shenandoah Valley, which would presumably keep Johnston from linking with Beauregard's ironically named Army of the Potomac (not to be confused with the Union's Army of the Potomac).

Beauregard

With his army divided in 3 columns, McDowell intended to use the bulk of his army, 2 columns, to make a diversionary feint at a couple of crossing points along Bull Run, while the third column crossed Bull Run a few miles away and came crashing down on one of Beauregard's flanks by surprise. With the third column marching on Beauregard's flank and in his rear, the outnumbered Confederates would be in danger of having their army's line of retreat cut off as well. If executed properly, McDowell assumed he could either bag Beauregard's army or force Beauregard to abandon Manassas Junction and fall back to the next defensible line, the Rappahannock River, which would ease the fears of Washington once the Confederates were no longer so close.

McDowell's strategy for the campaign was one tried by commanders on both sides throughout the war, and it would work successfully in the battle referred to as the Second Battle of Bull Run (Second Manassas). In August 1862, the Confederate Army of Northern Virginia under Robert E. Lee would decisively defeat John Pope's Union Army near Manassas by marching Stonewall Jackson's corps around Pope's right flank, waiting for Pope to throw his army at Jackson, and then rolling up Pope's left flank with a crushing assault by James Longstreet's corps. Unlike Lee, McDowell believed he could rely on a manpower advantage in July 1861.

Of course, Beauregard wasn't idle during this time either. When it became clear to him that McDowell was advancing, Beauregard began requesting reinforcements for his outnumbered Confederates, the most sensible being Johnston's men in the Shenandoah Valley. Beauregard was worried that he would be attacked in force on either the 18th or 19th, which would have prevented Johnston from linking up with his army.

McDowell's strategy during the First Battle of Bull Run was grand, and in many ways it was the forerunner of a tactic Lee and Jackson executed brilliantly in 1862. McDowell's plan called for parts of his army to pin down Confederate soldiers in front while marching another wing of his army around the flank and into the enemy's rear, rolling up the line. In July 1861, however, this proved far too difficult for his inexperienced troops to carry out effectively.

The First Battle of Bull Run made history in several ways. McDowell's army met Fort Sumter hero P.G.T. Beauregard's Confederate army near the railroad junction at Manassas on July 21, 1861. Located just 25 miles away from Washington D.C., many civilians from Washington came to watch what they expected to be a rout of Confederate forces. And for awhile, it appeared as though that might be the case.

When the Confederate line broke and ran south around 11:30 a.m., it appeared as though McDowell's plan was working perfectly. And had the attack taken place on July 19, Beauregard would've been unable to send reinforcements from Johnston, since they would still have been dozens of miles away with Joseph Johnston in the Shenandoah Valley. Instead, the Confederates could count on the inexperience of the Union attackers, who did not follow up their success on Matthews Hill and chase the Confederates up Henry Hill fast enough. This was due in part to an inexperienced commander as well; when the Confederate retreat was covered by John S. Imboden's artillery, McDowell instead held up his infantry's advance to bring up his own artillery, batteries led by James B. Ricketts (Battery I, 1st U.S. Artillery) and Charles Griffin (Battery D, 5th U.S.), and use them to attack the Confederates now reforming their line on Henry Hill. The delay allowed the Confederates to rally more reinforcements to their left on Henry Hill, including a brigadier general who was about to earn an eternal nickname.

McDowell's strategy fell apart thanks to railroads. Confederate reinforcements under General Joseph E. Johnston arrived by train in the middle of the day, a first in the history of American warfare, evening up the numbers between Union and Confederate. As the Confederates scrambled to fashion a new defensive line on Henry Hill, they were bolstered by the arriving brigade of Jackson, cavalry led by JEB Stuart, and Hampton's Legion, led by Wade Hampton III.

Jackson, since the inception of the brigade, stressed the importance of using the bayonet in battle as the majority of the C.S.A. Army had very short-ranged and grossly inaccurate muskets and balls, while the Union Army had the luxury of rifled bullets and gun barrels. Because of this, the defensive army, primarily the Confederates, had to hold fire until the enemy was close enough to be affected by the short-range muskets. This left the defenders in a safer position as the attackers were usually marching across an open field in an attempt to advance on the defenders. Fortifications and trenches were used throughout the war and holding the higher ground was imperative. Jackson once boasted, "My men sometimes fail to drive the enemy from his position, but to hold one, never."[15]

On July 21, Jackson rode along his men and ordered them to hold fire until the enemy was within 30 paces. The New York Zouaves, notable for their conspicuous red uniforms and tasseled hats, began their attack on Henry House Hill. Artillery was raining down and the entire Confederate left flank was under heavy fire. While troops from Mississippi, Alabama, Georgia, Louisiana, and South Carolina were falling back as ordered, Jackson's men held their ground. Private Casler recounted what happened next: "General Bernard E. Bee, riding up to General Jackson, who sat on his horse calm and unmoved, though severely wounded in the hand, exclaimed in a voice of anguish: 'General, they are beating us back.' Turning to General Bee, he said calmly: 'Sir, we'll give them the bayonet.' Hastening back to his men, General Bee cried enthusiastically, as he pointed to Jackson: 'Look yonder! There is Jackson and his brigade standing like a stone wall. Let us determine to die here and we will conquer. Rally behind them!'"[16]

Another account differed as it was said that Bee was in fact irritated by what appeared to be inactivity from Jackson and angrily gestured, "Look at Jackson standing there like a damned stone wall!" Either way, General Bee was mortally wounded shortly after that command and died the following day, so it remains unclear whether Bee was complimenting Jackson's brigade for standing firm or whether he was criticizing Jackson's brigade for being inactive on Henry Hill while the other Confederates were desperately defending and being pushed back.

Without Bee around to explain his command, nobody will ever know for certain, but that has not stopped people from debating Bee's comment. While Bee's comment might be interpreted as inaction, Jackson was badly wounded in the thick of the battle, ironically because he insisted on raising his arm during the battle, apparently as a result of his "unbalanced body" quirk. While doing that, his arm was hit by a bullet. Regardless, the nickname Stonewall stuck, and Jackson was henceforth known as Stonewall Jackson. His brigade also inherited the title, known throughout the war as the Stonewall brigade.

---

[15] Foner, 485.
[16] Casler, location 259-266.

Barnard Bee

Regardless of the true nature of Bee's comment, Jackson smartly protected his men by assembling them on the reverse slope of Henry Hill to protect them from enemy fire, while placing his guns on the crest of the hill where they could target the Union infantry and batteries. When the cannons were fired, the recoil would push them down the reverse slope, where the artillerymen could safely reload them, roll them back up, and repeat the process without exposing themselves to harm. Beauregard would later praise Jackson, "The conduct of General Jackson also requires mention as eminently that of an able, fearless soldier and sagacious commander, one fit to lead his efficient brigade. His prompt, timely arrival before the plateau of the Henry house, and his judicious disposition of his troops, contributed much to the success of the day. Although painfully wounded in the hand, he remained on the field to the end of the battle, rendering invaluable assistance."

With that, the fighting on Beauregard's left became an artillery duel, with Ricketts and Griffin operating 11 cannons against Jackson's 13, posted 300 yards away at the top of Henry Hill. While Jackson's batteries found their mark, most of the Union's shells overshot the Confederate infantry, which was good news for them but bad news for the Henry House, where handicapped 85 year old Judith Henry was stuck in bed and unable to evacuate. During the fighting, a shell crashed through her house and struck her leg, mortally wounding her.

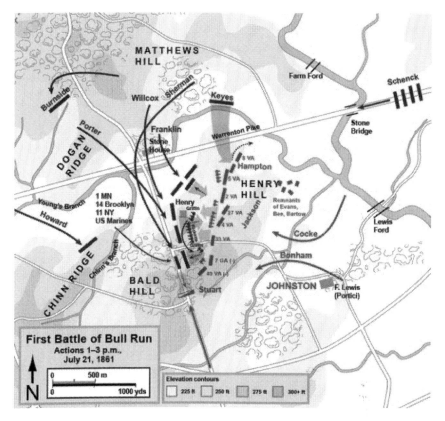

First Battle of Bull Run
Actions 1–3 p.m.,
July 21, 1861

Holding fire began to prove a difficult order as the New York Zouaves neared the Confederate left flank. Colonel Cummings, who commanded the 33rd, sensed the anticipatory nervousness of his men as the Zouaves initiated fire, but the Virginians maintained their position of lying in the prone position, thereby rendering the Union volley moot as the shots rang out over their heads.

After the first rounds were fired and Union artillery was spied within damaging range of the Confederates, Cummings, presumably of his own volition, ordered his men to fire then gave the command, "'Attention! Forward march! Charge bayonets! Double quick!'"[17] The 33rd charged down Henry House Hill with what came to be known as the trademark, "Rebel Yell," and began to sweep away everyone in their path.

---

[17] Casler, location 284.

The next stage of the fighting devolved into absolute chaos due to uniform colors. This had already presented a potential problem with some Union brigades, and while it caused confusion among the Confederates, it badly cost McDowell in the early afternoon. With his artillery in advanced position, around 3:00 p.m. Griffin's battery was overrun by the 33rd Virginia, which was wearing blue uniforms that Griffin's commander mistook for Union uniforms. Commanded not to fire on these blue-uniformed Confederates, Griffin's battery simply watched them march up and shatter them with a devastating volley from close range.

While fighting raged around the battery, the 33rd Virginia was supported by Stuart's cavalry, which rode right upon the right flank of the Union line, which consisted of the colorfully dressed Zouaves of the 11th New York. With this turn of luck, Jackson exploited the advantage by having two of his regiments charge and capture Ricketts's guns, leaving the positions of both Union batteries in Confederate hands.

While the fighting raged around the captured guns, the batteries changed hands several times, but the Union was unable to use its manpower advantage due to poor communication and inexperienced soldiers and officers. Though they still had double the Confederates' numbers, each Union advance was made piecemeal by no more than two regiments at a time, allowing the Confederates to repulse them from the advantage of the high ground. At the same time, Jackson continued to exhort his men to advance, sending the 4th Virginia down the hill with the orders, "Reserve your fire until they come within 50 yards! Then fire and give them the bayonet! And when you charge, yell like furies!"

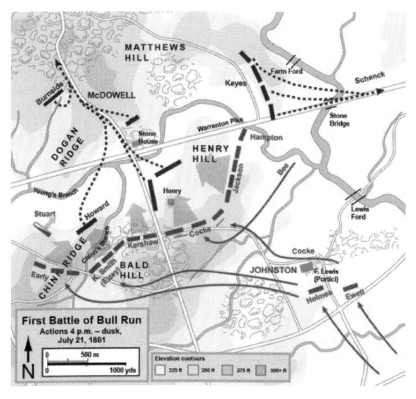

First Battle of Bull Run
Actions 4 p.m. – dusk,
July 21, 1861

Once again, inexperience ruled the day. As McDowell's army broke for the crossings back across Bull Run, they had to deal with obstacles like damaged wagons, Confederate artillery fire, and citizens who had come from Washington D.C. to watch what they anticipated would be a grand spectacle and Union victory. The fact that the crossings were narrow also caused the retreating Union soldiers to bottle up and get even more disorganized. Many of them could not be convinced to stop fleeing until they reached Washington D.C. itself over the next two days.

Thankfully for the Union army, the disorder of their flight was matched by the disorder of the Confederate chase. Beauregard himself had four horses shot out from under him during the fighting and at one point was left without a horse to pursue the retreating Union troops. Renowned historian William C. Davis noted that during the battle, "Beauregard acted chiefly as a dime novel general, leading the charge of an individual regiment, riding along the line to cheer the troops, accepting the huzzas of the soldiers and complementing them in turn."

Ultimately Beauregard called off the chase on the night of July 21, and with that he stirred an everlasting debate over whether or not he should have continued the pursuit. After the battle ended and the Union army was in rapid retreat, Beauregard stated sardonically that had Richmond dispatched adequate supplies to the Confederate armies, he would have been able to pursue the Union army all the way to Washington, implying that Davis had short-changed his troops and cost the Confederates an even greater victory. In his official report, which made its way into the newspapers, Beauregard suggested that Davis had prevented the pursuit and destruction of McDowell's army, as well as the potential capture of Washington D.C. itself. This only added to the animosity Davis already felt toward the celebrity-seeking general, and it would eventually lead to Beauregard being sidelined during the middle of the war. But as of July 21, 1861, Beauregard had won at Fort Sumter and First Bull Run, and Joseph Johnston, himself no fan of the Confederate president, also complained that lack of supplies had prevented his army from advancing against Washington. Furthermore, many cite Davis's "taking the field" at the Bull Run battlefield on July 21, 1861 as nothing more than a publicity stunt perpetuated by the headline-seeking Davis to insinuate a military role for himself as well.

As the first major battle of the Civil War, the First Battle of Bull Run was bound to be unprecedented and influential, but at the time it had several compelling effects on the generals and the politicians. For the leaders of the Union and the Confederacy, the battle not only served notice that the Civil War might be more protracted than they thought but also demonstrated the need for better organizing and drilling their armies, which acted more like mobs than professional soldiers at the battle.

Minor changes would be made as a result of confusion during the battle, including a change to the Confederates flag designs, but the battle also had far reaching effects on who would lead in the future. McDowell's Army of Northeastern Virginia would subsequently be integrated into the Army of the Potomac under the command of "The Young Napoleon", George McClellan, whose success in a campaign against Robert E. Lee in western Virginia early in the war seemed to verify everyone's belief that he was a prodigal general. McClellan would reorganize the Union armies around Washington into the largest military machine in the continent's history before striking out for Richmond on the Peninsula in early 1862. He would be opposed by Joseph Johnston, who retained command of the Confederate army, rechristened the Army of Northern Virginia in early 1862, and Johnston would fight McClellan until he was seriously injured at the Battle of Seven Pines and forced to turn command over to the legendary Robert E. Lee.

Out of all the men who fought at First Bull Run, however, the most important and best known was Stonewall Jackson. Jackson had been a virtual unknown upon his arrival at the front line of First Bull Run, but by the spring of 1862, Stonewall was already becoming known across battlefields. For its part, the 1st Virginia, which would become known as the Stonewall Brigade, took more casualties than any other brigade that day. More than 2,500 men took the field at the First Battle of Bull Run, with 373 suffering wounds and 111 being killed.[18] Numerous men from the 33rd, who were primarily responsible for holding the left flank of the battle line, died on the field, including John Casler's friend, William Blue. His regiment entered the battle with "450 men, and lost forty-three killed and 140 wounded."[19]

After the battlefield fell silent, Casler walked among the dead to see which of his friends had been killed. This is when he discovered the body of William Blue lying face down on the cluttered field. He rolled his friend onto his back and determined that he had been killed instantly while in the process of loading his musket as he had "one hand grasped around the gun, in the other he held a cartridge, with one end of it in his mouth, in the act of tearing it off."[20] Casler sat on the ground beside his friend and cried, though he told himself it was not something a soldier should do. He slept for the night on the once thunderous field and when he awoke the following morning, his regiment was ordered to fall-in and prepare to depart for an unknown destination. Casler hid while the remainder of the men assembled in formation and stayed behind to honor his promise to his dead friend. William I. Blue was buried that morning under a tree near Henry House Hill.

Chapter 3: The Valley Campaign and the Seven Days Battles

The following months consisted of camp life and picket duty for Casler and his mates. They maintained camps in and around Centerville, not far from Alexandria. It was in October that the C.S.A. government created the Department of Northern Virginia and promoted Thomas Jackson to Major General with orders to report to Winchester and assume command of the Shenandoah Valley District. By this time, the Stonewall Brigade was part of Joseph Johnston's Army of Northern Virginia.

The men were distraught at the news of losing their stern but beloved leader. Jackson's troops, who primarily hailed from the Shenandoah Valley, were disheartened that they were unable to accompany the general. Before leaving, Jackson assembled his brigade to bid them this farewell:

> "Officers and Soldiers of the First Brigade: I am not here to make a speech, but simply to say farewell. I first met you at Harper's Ferry, in the commencement of this war, and I cannot take leave of you without giving expression to my admiration for your conduct from that day to this, whether on the march, the bivouac, the tented field, or the bloody plains of Manassas, when you gained the well deserved reputation of having decided the fate of

---

[18] Smith, 22. It is important to note that a high number of those wounded during the Civil War eventually succumbed to their injuries. Those that later died away from military hospitals were not counted among the dead of the war. This was especially true for the Confederacy as many of their records were burned when they evacuated Richmond. Also, during the war period, the North had the means by which to procure medications for their wounded whereas the South was only able to supply medicine that was snuck through the southern ports by blockade runners.

[19] Casler, location 314.

[20] Casler, location 302.

that battle.

"Throughout the broad extent of country over which you have marched, by your respect for the rights and property of citizens you have shown that you were soldiers, not only to defend, but able and willing to both defend and protect. You have already gained a brilliant and deservedly high reputation throughout the army and the whole Confederacy, and I trust in the future, by your own deeds on the field, and by the assistance of the same kind Providence who has heretofore favored our cause, you will gain more victories, and add additional luster to the reputation you now enjoy.

"You have already gained a proud position in the future history of this, our second war of independence. I shall look with great anxiety to your future movements, and I trust that whenever I shall hear of the 1st Brigade on the field of battle it will be of still nobler deeds achieved and a higher reputation won.

"In the Army of the Shenandoah you were the *First* Brigade, in the Army of the Potomac you were the *First* Brigade, in the 2d Corps of this army you are the *First* Brigade; you are *First* Brigade in the affections of your general, and I hope by your future deeds and bearing you will be handed down to posterity as the *First* Brigade in this, our second war of independence. Farewell!"[21]

As it turned out, this moving speech was premature in its deliverance, because just one month later, after witnessing the deplorable troops over who he was to command, Jackson called for his old brigade to reinforce him in the Valley.

An unusual strategic aspect of the Civil War was that the opposing nations' capitals were little more than a hundred miles apart and connected by good roads. That distance amounted to only four days' hard marching, or one grueling cavalry ride. This proximity meant that protecting their respective capitals dominated the strategic thinking on both sides. Large numbers of men had to stay close to the capitals in order to protect them, and any major operations in the Eastern Theater had to take this into account.

Another geographic factor also played a major role. 100 miles to the west of Richmond, running from the northeast to the southwest, are the Blue Ridge Mountains, a formidable barrier to travel, but with several passes through which an army could pass. This mountain chain runs along almost the entire length of western Virginia and reaches to a point almost parallel with Washington, DC. Beyond the Blue Ridge Mountains lies the Shenandoah Valley, an abundant agricultural zone. Not only did the Valley offer plentiful supplies for whatever side controlled it,

---

[21] Casler, location 678-691.

but the Valley acted as a protected corridor along which an army could move in to flank the opposing capital.

At the beginning of 1862, the Confederacy controlled most of the Shenandoah Valley, which put the local Confederate army, based at Winchester, uncomfortably close to Washington. In the early months of that year, Jackson was given command of an army numbering about 17,000 in the Shenandoah Valley. His task was daunting. The loss at Bull Run prompted a changing of the guard, with George B. McClellan, the "Young Napoleon", put in charge of reorganizing and leading the Army of the Potomac. That spring, the Army of the Potomac conducted an ambitious amphibious invasion of Virginia's peninsula, circumventing the Confederate defenses to the north of Richmond by attacking Richmond from the southeast. General Johnston's outnumbered army headed toward Richmond to confront McClellan, but the Union still had three armies totaling another 50,000 around the Shenandoah Valley, which represented a threat to Richmond from the north. It was these armies that Jackson would be tasked with stopping. Confederate president Jefferson Davis ruefully observed, "The military paradox, that impossibilities must be rendered possible, had never better occasion for its application."

In regards to the Shenandoah Valley, McClellan knew that Jackson's force was relatively small, so he only sent 16,000 men under the command of Major General Nathaniel P. Banks. A former Speaker of the House and Governor of Massachusetts, Banks was one of the many "political" generals Lincoln had raised to command at the beginning of the war, in spite of the fact that his only real military credentials were that his Massachusetts militia were considered some of the best in the North. Banks himself had no real combat experience.

Nathaniel Banks

Erring on the side of caution, McClellan sent a couple more brigades to act as a reserve for Banks. This included 6,000 men under Brigadier General John Sedgwick, who had joined him at Harpers Ferry, and 5,000 men under Brigadier General Alpheus Williams, who had secured Martinsburg on the Baltimore & Ohio Railroad further to the northwest. Another 15,000 men under General Frederick Lander were supposed to move down to meet Williams at Martinsburg, but on March 2, Lander died of a lingering illness leaving his army stopped in confusion.

Banks' main objective was to guard the capital's flank and tie Jackson down so he couldn't help the Confederate center when protecting Richmond. If possible, he would destroy the rebels in the Valley and secure it for the Union, which would open up the possibility of attacking Richmond from the west. On February 26, his enlarged force began crossing the Potomac River at Harpers Ferry on a temporary pontoon bridge. The advance on Winchester was delayed for some time in order to strengthen the bridge, which was bending in the middle, and to rebuild the old Baltimore & Ohio Railroad Bridge that had been destroyed the previous year. The bigger, stronger bridge would be vital in order to allow large numbers of men to safely pass.

For his part, Jackson was ordered to tie up as many Union troops as possible in the Valley to keep them away from the main center of the fight. Considering the disparity in numbers, that was asking a great deal.

The first thing the rebel general did was to fall back south 50 miles to his supply depot at Mt. Jackson. This allowed him room to maneuver against the superior force arrayed against him (although at this point he wasn't aware just how great the disparity between the two forces was), and he would be able to move east through one of the passes in the Blue Ridge Mountains to help Johnson at Centreville if need be.

By the time Jackson finally abandoned Winchester on March 12 in the face of the Union advance, he had decided not to retreat too far south. The withdrawal had begun to affect morale, and Jackson was still hoping to find a way to strike at the federals, so he ordered a withdrawal only eighteen miles south to Strasburg. There he stayed for several days, gathering supplies and hearing the welcome news that thousands of men had been scraped together to come to his aid. Meanwhile, the federals didn't follow. Their prime goal was to seal off the Valley, keep Jackson from flanking the Army of the Potomac, and get at Washington, which they had already accomplished.

By March 16, Jackson had retreated almost to Mt. Jackson. This greatly shortened his supply lines and helped get reinforcements to him more quickly, but to his dismay, they came into camp in a piecemeal fashion, a few hundred at a time. Even worse, most were conscripts, poorly trained, and poorly armed. Some weren't armed at all. Another problem was that many of the local recruits were Mennonites, Quakers, and members of other pacifist religious groups. These people were opposed to slavery and war, making them singularly unqualified to fight in the Confederate army. Jackson realized that while he could force rifles into their hands, he couldn't force them to shoot accurately, so he made them teamsters and medical staff.

The first major battle of the Valley Campaign was at Kernstown on March 23, 1862. It was a Sunday, and Jackson, a devoutly Christian man, didn't want to fight on the Sabbath, but he changed his mind when he saw the lay of the land. Not far off from Pritchard's Hill was Sandy Ridge, which offered a similarly good view of the Valley. He rushed the Stonewall Brigade, under the command of Brigadier General Richard Garnett, to this ridge, where a stone wall offered them protection. The Union troops saw the opportunity too, and raced to get there first.

One rebel soldier remembered, "It was 'nip and tuck' which would reach it first, but the 37th Virginia got there first, and, kneeling down, poured a deadly volley into the other at close quarters and nearly annihilated it. Such would have been their fate if the Federals had gotten their first."

When the Union troops fell back, Jackson rushed artillery to this important position.

The artillery on Pritchard's Hill and Sandy Ridge dueled for a time, then, around 4 p.m., Col. Kimball ordered a division of Ohio troops to take the ridge. They advanced under the shelter of the woods for a time, taking harassing fire from skirmishers, until they emerged from the tree line and traveled down a gentle descent into a ravine.

As soon as the Ohio men came into sight, the Stonewall Brigade opened up on them with their artillery and rifles. Captain George L. Wood of the 7th Ohio later wrote of this onslaught, "The grape and canister was tearing bark from the tree over our heads, while the solid shot and shell made great gaps in their trunks. Under our feet the turf was being torn up, and around and about us the air was thick with flying missiles. Not a gun was fired on our side. The head of the column soon reached the ravine, when a deafening discharge of musketry greeted us. A sheet of flame shot along the stone wall, followed by an explosion that shook the earth, and the missiles tore through the solid ranks of the command with a fearful certainty."

The Ohioans hid in the ravine, trying to find whatever cover they could. Some fired back, while others simply hid. The officers had trouble enough protecting themselves, let alone organizing their men. The Union reserve line on the low rise behind the ravine tried to give covering fire, but some of the bullets fell short and into the ravine. Corporal Selden Day recalled, "Men were falling all around me, and glancing backward I saw that the slope of the hill was barely sufficient to enable the men in the rear to fire safely over the heads of those of us in the front. A sergeant of Company H fell near me, shot through the neck, and I was quite sure it was done from the rear."

As their numbers grew, the Ohioans regained their nerve. They tried to advance, and took heavy losses, but also inflicted some on the enemy. Kimball fed more men into the fight, both on the front and on the rebels' right flank. Although these attacks were pushed aside, Garnett's men began running low on ammunition. The flanking attack came back with renewed strength, and the men defending the wall began to waver. Then came a Union cavalry attack on the rebel left. General Garnett, fearing envelopment, ordered his men to withdraw.

A determined rearguard action allowed the rest of the rebels to retreat five miles south into the twilight. The close of day stopped the hostilities.

General Banks saw that Jackson meant business, and so recalled General Williams' brigade that was en route to Centreville. The rebels suffered 139 killed, 312 wounded, and 253 captured.

The Union lost 118, 450 were wounded, and 22 were missing or captured. The Pritchard home was turned into a hospital, with Samuel, the pregnant Helen, and their children aiding the groaning and bleeding men of both sides.

Though Stonewall Jackson had lost the battle, he gained a strategic victory by draining troops from the main fight in front of Richmond; the Valley Campaign had begun in earnest.

Although Jackson is revered today as an almost ideal commander, a lot of his subordinates bristled under his leadership, believing not only that he asked too much but that he was too strict. One of the first to feel Jackson's wrath was General Garnett, who led the Stonewall Brigade at Kernstown. When Garnett retreated from a bad position without orders during the battle because his men were running low on ammunition, Jackson had him arrested, and he was later court-martialed. Jackson had essentially questioned Garnett's manhood, humiliating him, and for the rest of the war, Garnett would try to prove his courage. Although he could not walk after being kicked by a horse in the days before the Battle of Gettysburg, Garnett famously insisted on riding a horse at the head of his brigade during Pickett's Charge, which made him a very conspicuous target. Garnett was killed during the charge.

Garnett

After the battle of Kernstown, Stonewall Jackson once again withdrew his men to Mt. Jackson. Union forces shadowed him for a time, but there were no engagements. Once safely south, Jackson focused on getting more conscripts. Enraged at General Garnett for retreating at Kernstown without orders, he relieved him of duty. The rank and file, however, saw Garnett as saving his battered regiments, who were almost out of ammunition, from being overwhelmed by the Yankees. As a result, Jackson's stern decision was unpopular and bad for morale, but the men would, however, soon have something else to focus on.

In Washington, Stonewall Jackson's bold attack was having the desired effect: Lincoln had decided to send more men to the Shenandoah Valley. He was also concerned about the safety of Washington from Confederate forces directly to the south of the capital, and reserved more men from McClellan's planned offensive to protect the city. Lincoln also reduced McClellan's command, breaking the Army of the Potomac into three departments. McClellan was to remain in command of the 67,000 troops headed to the Virginia Peninsula. The Department of the Rappahannock under General Irvin McDowell was entrusted with protecting the capital and the area to the south.

On April 30, Jackson moved his men out of Swift Run Gap to meet him there. Banks wasn't far north in Harrisonburg with 19,000 men, but he wasn't in a position to attack. When he finally discovered Jackson's location, Lincoln ordered him to withdraw north to Strasburg. The President worried that Banks had extended his supply lines too far and had left the capital's western flank exposed, and Jackson was able to move to Staunton unopposed. In the meantime, Ewell had moved into Jackson's old camp at Swift Run Gap. Banks learned of this move as well, and realized he had a much larger force of rebels to contend with than before.

Jackson linked up with Johnson, and with 10,000 men, continued west to the town of McDowell, 30 miles west of Staunton, where Union Brigadier General Milroy was headed with 6,000 Union troops. Jackson saw this as an opportunity to locally outnumber a Union force and defeat it before it could be reinforced.

After a long lull in the campaign in which both sides slogged through heavy rainfall on bad roads, they were finally about to meet in battle. On May 7, Jackson's enlarged army came into sight of Milroy's smaller one, but the battle did not start well for the rebels. The Confederate vanguard came over Shenandoah Mountain on the Staunton & Parkersburg Turnpike and was surprised by Union artillery barrage. The rebels wavered, but as more of Jackson's force came into view, Milroy lost his nerve and withdrew to McDowell, moving so quickly he left much of his army's camp gear behind. He sent desperate word to Fremont to for reinforcements, but the only ones close enough to help were the 1,500 men under General Robert Schenck. Milroy would still be outnumbered.

Both Union commanders feared that the rebels would bring artillery to the top of Sitlington's Hill. From there, the Valley, the town, and the Union soldiers in it would look like a bull's-eye in the middle of a target, so Milroy convinced Union general Schenck to give him 2,300 men to take to the hill In fact, the rebels did not bring artillery to the top of the hill because Jackson found the going too rough, and he feared that a determined Union attack would capture the guns before they could withdraw.

Unaware of Jackson's decision, Schenck agreed to give Milroy the men, and at around 3 p.m., Milroy and his men moved out, to work their way up the ravines on the west side of Sitlington's Hill. In back of them, the Union artillery dug ditches behind their guns in order to increase the elevation of the barrels, and to offer covering fire for their comrades as they clambered up the hill.

Given the disparity in numbers, the terrain, and the impossibility of defending the town, there was no real chance of the battle going any other way. That night, the little Union army headed north towards Franklin, 30 miles away. Jackson had forced the enemy to retreat, but he feared that Fremont might move east and link up with Banks at Harrisonburg. To delay this, he sent a detachment of cavalry to destroy bridges and block roads between Franklin and Harrisonburg. Jackson himself cautiously moved towards Franklin in the hope of hitting the Federals again.

Meanwhile, Confederate General Richard S. Ewell was becoming increasingly impatient at being told to remain at Swift Run Gap. He wanted to get into the fight, but the fight seemed to be passing him by. He had hoped to fight the Union forces gathering at Fredericksburg when he was on the east side of the Blue Ridge Mountains. Then he had been ordered into the Shenandoah, only to be left in Jackson's old camp as Jackson ran around the Valley, fooling the Yankees. Ewell wasn't even sure where Jackson was at that time, and he complained, loudly, about Jackson's lack of communication, even snapping at one of his colonels, "I tell you sir, he is as crazy as a March Hare! He has gone away, I don't know where, and left me here with instructions to stay until he returns. But Banks' whole army is advancing on me, and I have not the most remote idea where to communicate with General Jackson. I tell you, sir, he is crazy, and I will just march my division away from here. I do not mean to have it cut to pieces at the behest of a crazy man."

Though he was still unclear on the Confederate movements, Banks suspected they might be coming, and requested permission to withdraw further up the Valley. When his request was refused, he dug in and sent 900 men of the 1st Maryland to Front Royal to protect his left flank and rear. General Fremont's force of 15,000 was still far away at Franklin and was not able to come to his aid. Jackson had 10,000 men and Ewell had 8,000, and together they outnumbered every Union army in the area as long as they kept the Yankees separated. With Shields on his way out of the Valley and Col. Ashby's cavalry on the road ready to harass Fremont if he advanced, it looked like Jackson would have Banks all to himself.

Once again, Stonewall Jackson's better intelligence gathering helped him. He had heard of the detachment at Front Royal and decided to hit it with his superior numbers. The Union men at Front Royal were the 1st Maryland. Jackson also had a regiment of 1st Maryland (Confederate). Maryland was a border state, and like all border states, it had regiments in both armies. This was the case with the Southern states as well. When the war broke out, loyalists from all across the South formed their own Union regiments. These were often quickly crushed, or had to flee to the North and fight far from their home territories. Others stayed dormant until the main Union army approached, at which point they rallied to the Stars and Stripes. In fact, every state in the Confederacy had provided loyal regiments to the Union army.

The 1st Maryland (Confederate) was in almost as much trouble as the 1st Maryland (Union). While the boys in blue were about to face an overwhelming force, their neighbors in gray were suffering from low morale. Their terms of enlistment were almost up and they had grown tired of slogging through cold rains and daily marches on muddy roads. Some of them wanted to go home. Others wanted to join the cavalry. The more disciplined among them felt obliged to disarm the troublemakers and keep a close eye on them in case they mutinied.

Jackson wanted to capture all the defenders of Front Royal, so on May 23, he decided on a double envelopment. Ewell led a large force that included the 1st Maryland (Confederate) to the east of town, while Ashby and his veteran cavalry cut west. Ashby had the double duty of keeping an eye on Banks at Strasburg, 12 miles away. Jackson came straight forward at Front Royal with the bulk of his men.

Oddly, Jackson sent the 1st Maryland (Confederate) in first. They were under strength, numbering only about 350, and many men had to be given back their weapons on the promise of good behavior, but at the sign of a fight the rebel Marylanders seemed to pluck up their spirits.

The 1st Maryland (Union) was caught completely by surprise, as they had assumed Jackson was miles away. When they realized the whole rebel army would follow, they fell back to Richardson's Hill to the north of town, firing their artillery at the charging rebels. Soon more Confederates appeared, closing in on all sides, and the Unionist Marylanders burnt their camp and fled across the bridges to the north of town.

This was followed by an inexplicable lull in the fighting. The Confederates had taken the town, but seemed slow to advance on a strong position protected by artillery. Their hesitation gave the Union troops time to pile hay on the bridges and set them alight.

Jackson immediately saw the danger. Time was of the essence in this campaign, and he could not afford to spend days building bridges when he needed to be able to move north at a moment's notice. He ordered his men forward, under fire, to toss the burning hay bales into the rushing water below.

They barely stopped the fire in time. Even so, the flames had badly damaged the bridges and the men hesitated to cross them. Impatient, Jackson ordered Major Thomas Flournoy to take his 250 troopers in the 6th Virginia Cavalry across the bridge and hit the enemy hard. They made it across in spite of the weakened planks, and began a running fight with the Yankees, lasting almost 3 miles before they had them trapped and were able to charge through their lines.

Back in Washington, Lincoln was seriously concerned. Exaggerated reports came in that Jackson had 20,000 men, which meant that the capital itself might be in danger. The president telegraphed Fremont, saying, "The exposed condition of General Banks makes his immediate relief a point of paramount importance. You are therefore directed by the President to move against Jackson at Harrisonberg [sic] and operate against the enemy in such way as to relieve Banks. This movement must be made immediately. You will acknowledge the receipt of this order and specify the hour it is received by you."

The beleaguered president had all too much experience with hesitant generals, and this last sentence was Lincoln's way to ensure Fremont responded quickly. But even if the slow-moving Fremont had responded with unusual alacrity, he would take some time to get there, so Lincoln turned to General McDowell and his 41,000 troops who were threatening Richmond in the center. He ordered McDowell to detach 20,000 men, nearly half his force, and move them into the Shenandoah Valley, which meant that any direct assault against Richmond would have to wait. McClellan, who was hoping to link up with McDowell on the northeast part of the Peninsula to provide a united front against the rebel capital, grew even more uncertain.

McDowell protested the order and noted, "If the enemy can succeed so readily in disconcerting all our plans by alarming us first at one point, then at another, he will paralyze a large force with a very small one." Here, for once, was a Union commander who quite clearly saw that of which Jackson was capable.

By the night of May 24, Banks was just south of Winchester. He decided to rest there and offer battle the next day. He only had 6,500 men and was badly outnumbered, but was now in a better position and he wanted to give his 550 remaining supply wagons a chance to make it to Williamsport on the Potomac River 35 miles away. To lose those would be disastrous. The Confederate armies were chronically short of supplies through much of the war and often tried to capture Union wagon trains.

Stonewall Jackson arrived at dawn the next day. He peered through the mist, to observe the hastily dug fortifications in front of him and decided to attack at once. He ordered Ewell to attack the Union's left flank, where Banks had positioned only 1,000 men. He ordered Brigadier General Dick Taylor, in command of a Louisiana brigade known as the "Louisiana Tigers," to go after the Union's right flank. As usual, Jackson placed himself in the center.

The fog slowly thinned. The artillery on both sides dueled as the rebels moved forward to get into position. When visibility had increased enough to attack, the Confederate flanks hit the Union army hard, letting loose with a wild, rebel yell.

The Union defense crumpled. Jackson ordered his men forward to charge the Union center, but by the time he had arrived they were already withdrawing. The Union troops fled through Winchester, leaving almost all their supplies behind. Jackson urged his men forward, hoping to trap Banks between his own forces and the Potomac, and wipe him out as Banks had wiped out the detachment at Front Royal.

Jackson's attack did not go to plan: Ashby had disappeared, Ewell's cavalry was too mired in the chaos of battle to provide a solid fighting force until two in the afternoon, and his foot soldiers were unable to keep up with the fleeing federals.

The fighting between Front Royal and the rout at Winchester cost the Union army dearly. They saw 71 killed, 243 wounded, and 1,714 missing (about 800 of whom were captured). The supply depot at Winchester contained nearly 10,000 small arms, half a million rounds of ammunition, two rifled cannons, $250,000 in medial supplies, some 25,000 pounds of rations, and more than 100 head of cattle, all of which fell into rebel hands. Jackson's army had saw 68 killed, 329 wounded, and 3 missing.

Banks headed out of the Valley, and for the moment, Jackson had the Shenandoah Valley to himself. More importantly, Jackson had made enough of a fuss to pull Shields's men and some 20,000 of General McDowell's troops out of Fredericksburg. The Union center, which only days before had been poised to strike a deathly blow at Richmond, was now too weak for offensive operations. On the Virginia Peninsula, McClellan was still indecisive and moving slowly. Lincoln wrote to him in despair, "I think the time is near when you must either attack Richmond or give up the job and come to the defense of Washington."

The Union's plan to take Richmond, and perhaps end the war after only a year, was in tatters. Now that the center of the fighting had shifted towards the Shenandoah, Lincoln wanted Jackson and his spirited little army to be severely punished. If the Union could take and hold the Shenandoah Valley, it would salvage something out of the season's disaster. Just as the Shenandoah flanked Washington, it flanked Richmond. Controlling it would give the North another chance at the Confederate capital.

Shields was already on his way with McDowell's force just behind them. Lincoln also urged Fremont to move to help Banks. Fremont noted that the "bridges and culverts had been destroyed, rocks rolled down, and in one instance trees felled across the way for the distance of nearly a mile," meaning that Ashby's cavalry and local rebel sympathizers had wrecked the roads. Still, he managed to move his army forward, leaving behind their personal baggage and tents in an effort to move quickly enough to save Banks, who had fled across the Potomac to Williamsport, Maryland.

After the Battle of Winchester, Jackson allowed his men two days of rest and prayer, while his quartermasters tallied the spoils left behind by the Yankees. Although Jackson drove his men hard, he could sense they were at their limit; their failure to pursue Banks' broken army was proof of it. While he was eager to get on with the fight, he needed men capable of fighting.

He finally set out on May 28, headed for Harpers Ferry at the confluence of the Shenandoah and Potomac rivers. The Union High Command guessed he was coming, and rushed 7,000 men under General Rufus Saxton to guard the town. Saxon placed an advanced guard of 1,500 of his troops at Charlestown, seven miles west of Harpers Ferry, to watch for the rebels. Jackson's vanguard came upon them and forced them back to Harpers Ferry after a mere twenty minutes of artillery bombardment. The rest of Jackson's army didn't arrive on the scene until after dark.

Meanwhile, to Jackson's rear, the federals were closing in. Shields approached Front Royal with 10,000 men. This lay along Jackson's main route of retreat and was held only by a single regiment—the 12th Georgia under Colonel Z.T. Conner. For some inexcusable reason, perhaps overconfidence over the successes of the recent campaign, Conner hadn't bothered to put out enough pickets, and didn't know of Shields's approach until just before he started shelling the camp.

Shields struck at around 11:30; the soldiers from Georgia had no choice but to beat a hasty retreat. They stayed just long enough to torch the captured Union supplies, but left behind about 500 Union prisoners, recently captured at the Battle of Front Royal.

Jackson withdrew that same day. He shelled Harpers Ferry and drove the defenders out of town and out of range, but he didn't dare attack. He had heard McDowell and Fremont were on their way, and needed to get out before a brilliant campaign turned into a disaster. The Valley Turnpike was the only one safe road for him to take. If McDowell managed to cut it off, he'd be trapped. He once again ordered his men on a long, grueling march. His men had gone on so many of these that Jackson affectionately referred to his men as his "foot cavalry." Now they would have to move faster than ever.

Leaving the Stonewall Brigade temporarily behind to create a diversion to cover the army's retreat, Jackson led the rest of his men on a hard march south. The evening of May 31 found them at Strasburg. Jackson was surprised to find the city free from Union troops. He sent scouts out and discovered that Fremont was only four miles to their west, dealing with Ashby's cavalry, desperately trying to slow their advance. Shields's force was at Front Royal only ten miles southeast.

What Jackson didn't know was that Fremont and Shields were not in communication, and did not know each other's position or intention. In addition, they both thought Jackson's army was far larger than it actually was, and proceeded with caution.

Jackson knew this lucky state of affairs would not last for long, but he had to wait for the Stonewall Brigade. He formed up his men, sent Ewell's men to the west to watch for Fremont's advance, and moved himself to the east to avoid Shields, in case he got curious about what was going on in Strasburg, and then he and his men settled down for a nervous night's sleep.

The next day was a Sunday, a day on which Jackson would rather not fight, but perhaps he felt he was being helped by a higher power, after all the recent rain, which had seen the Union pursuit bogged down on the muddy roads.

Ewell spent the morning skirmishing with Fremont's men, while the Union general showed no inclination to advance and bring on a battle. The Stonewall Brigade arrived around noon, and Jackson ordered both flanks to break off and head south. They had managed to slip by the federals once again, although it wouldn't be long before they would feel them nipping at their heels.

By June 8, Stonewall Jackson had made it to Port Republic with his vanguard, but his weary army was still stretched out for several miles along the road behind him. In the rearguard were Ewell and 5,000 men at Cross Keys, a crossroads hamlet with a few houses and a tavern as its namesake. It was hazardous for Jackson to have his smaller army so divided, but with the state of his men, it couldn't be helped.

The Battle of Cross Keys

Jackson was preparing for Sunday services early that morning, when he had a scare in the form of some blue-coated riders charging up the road from the east, headed straight for his supply wagons. These were positioned east of the hamlet, which was separated from Port Republic by two rivers--the North River and the South River--which formed the South Fork of the Shenandoah River. In actuality, the North and South Forks are misnamed, as they actually run west and east. Having passed the rough, almost impassible massif, the South (east) Fork was all that stood between Jackson's army and the approaching force under Shields. Jackson was himself in town, but most of his men were to the west of it. As the riders came in, the rebel general hurried away to avoid being captured. Some of his personal staff, however, were not as lucky.

Though the Union cavalry numbered a mere 150 men, they were poised to strike Jackson's army a killing blow. All they had to do was burn the bridge over the rivers, and the rebels would be separated from their supply wagons, and cut off from further retreat. This represented a potential turning point in the war, and they didn't take it. Whether it was because the federals had been too hampered over the past few weeks by burned bridges to burn one themselves, or because their commander, a mere colonel, didn't want to take the responsibility on himself, the moment slipped away.

The morning of June 9 dawned cool and foggy. Ewell's men were on the road again, this time to march to Port Republic to help Stonewall Jackson deal with the Union army under Shields. So confident was Jackson, that Fremont would not attack that morning. Instead, he ordered Ewell to leave only a single brigade behind to hold Fremont's army at bay. The rebel generals hoped to defeat Shields and return to Cross Keys to finish off Fremont.

It was a bold plan that required swift movement. The problem was that swift movement was impossible. The only bridge across the South Fork had been hastily thrown up by the rebels, who were short on nails, and the boards that lay across it were mostly loose. As the men marched across it in the predawn gloom, they kept knocking the boards out of place, forcing those behind them to waste their time setting them back into place.

The Stonewall Brigade made it over first, but it was apparent that the others would take some time. Jackson, growing impatient, led his one brigade forward. Two brigades of Shields's force, led by Brigadier Generals Erastus B. Tyler and Samuel Carroll, waited ahead in the darkness. Two more brigades, led by Shields himself, were still farther up the road, and not in an immediate position to help.

The Union troops were little over a mile from the rickety bridge. They had found a good position atop a large hill which had been stripped of its trees to make charcoal and upon which seven Union cannons now sat. Nine more cannons were arrayed in other places along the line. The Union troops, numbering some 3,500 men, had anchored their left flank to this hill and their right flank on the river. They were twice Jackson's number in size.

At around 5 a.m., Jackson split his inferior force into two. Half of the Stonewall Brigade went straight for the federal guns, while the other half moved through the cover of the underbrush to come at the Union's left flank, with the h ope of creeping up the hill to grab their artillery. The Stonewall Brigade was supported by some rebel artillery, but the advance faltered when they ran out of ammunition.

Just then, a second rebel brigade of Louisianans showed up. With the fight a little more even, Jackson ordered another attack. This time the rebels advanced to within 200 yards of the Union line, but had to hide behind a fence to save themselves from the heavy fire, only to withdraw an hour later. The Union troops rushed after them.

Jackson realized that his army may very well be trapped. He sent a message to the brigade facing Fremont to make all haste to join the fight, burning the bridges after them to keep Fremont from following. Though this would cut off the rebels' line of retreat, Jackson had no choice but to take the chance and defeat Shields, or be annihilated.

A third rebel brigade under General Ewell arrived. He hit the advancing Yankees in the flank, stopping them in their tracks. Another quick, flanking maneuver caught the guns on the hill unawares, and the rebels managed to capture six of them. The Union troops wasted no time in their counterattack, and the hilltop turned into a free-for-all of stabbing bayonets, clubbed rifles, and slashing swords. Confederate general Dick Taylor recalled that the Union gunners defended their cannons with "their rammers in a way not laid down in the Manual…'Twas claw for claw." After a bitter fight, the Louisianans were beaten back, leaving a horrid scene that a soldier of the 13th Virginia described as: "Men in grey and those in blue piled up in front of and around the guns and with horses dying and the blood of men and beasts flowing almost in a stream."

By then, two more of Jackson's brigades had shown up, as well as some additional artillery. Under cover of a heavy fire, Jackson threw his men into a massive assault. The Union line faltered, and then withdrew in order. The battle was over. Generals Tyler and Carroll marched 8 miles north to Conrad's Store, where they reunited with Shields. Their commander decided not to run the risk of being defeated twice in the same day and had the men take up defensive positions. Jackson, of course, wasted no time attacking him, and then headed for safety, no doubt sending up a prayer of thanks for having his army delivered from destruction.

Casualties were roughly equal on both sides. The Union saw 94 killed, 406 wounded, and 603 missing or captured. The Confederacy had 239 killed, 928 wounded, and 96 missing or captured. Shields, however, had decisively lost the battle, and Jackson had gotten what he needed—a passage to safety.

Neither federal army was in any condition to chase them. They had marched too long, and been defeated too often. It must have come as a relief to Shields to receive orders from Lincoln to move east to Fredericksburg to join the position directly between Richmond and Washington. It would mean more marching and more fighting, but at least they would be leaving the Shenandoah Valley. Fremont was also ordered to withdraw and return to Harrisonburg, but the general felt this was too close to the rebel army to hold securely, so he asked permission to retreat 25 miles further north to Mt. Jackson. He set out in that direction before getting a reply.

As a final, bitter twist, the orders to pull back were dated before the battles of Cross Keys and

Port Republic; the final two defeats had been for nothing.

For the moment, Shields could rest as he waited for Banks to march all the way from Winchester to Front Royal in order to take his position. Shields urgently requested supplies, including a large number of shoes, since one of every three of his men were barefoot. Fremont wasn't much better off. His army had dwindled to about 10,000 effectives; the rest were too exhausted to fight. His men were also short of shoes, and most of the army's horses were worn out. Many of the artillery horses were so weak, they could no longer pull their cannons.

Jackson, on the other hand, would be reinforced with several regiments, bringing his total force to 18,500. Robert E. Lee wrote to tell him, "Your recent successes have been the cause of the liveliest joy in this army as well as in the country." He added that the reinforcements were so he could crush the Union armies in the Shenandoah, unaware at this point they were in the process of being recalled. Jackson was to leave the Valley and support the Confederate center above Richmond by cutting Union communications.

Jackson received these orders on June 16, and immediately prepared to move out. On the 18th, the army headed south in the direction of the Blue Ridge Mountains and Waynesboro, where trains waited to take them to Richmond, where they would find a situation that had changed remarkably little. The Union center, poised above Richmond, had been too weakened by reinforcements sent to the Shenandoah Valley to make a proper assault on the Confederate capital. On the Virginia Peninsula, McClellan still dawdled, continuously asking for more troops and more supplies. Repeated requests from Washington to do something, anything, were met with replies that the weather was unfavorable or there weren't yet enough troops. He already had 130,000 men, which was the figure he'd requested when he first planned this campaign, but now he asked for 100,000 more. McClellan, always hesitant in the face of the enemy, was outdoing even himself.

By June 23, riding far ahead of his men, Stonewall Jackson arrived at General Lee's headquarters, just outside Richmond. That same day he'd participated in a discussion about Lee's plan to concentrate forces and hit the Union army above Richmond in their right flank. The plan was to bring to bear 56,000 troops against a single corps, break it, and roll up the line in order to push the right flank, and then all of McClellan's army, away from Richmond and down the Peninsula. It was a plan that Jackson could have thought up himself—focusing as many men as possible in one area in order to get numerical superiority.

While Jackson was practically performing a miracle in the Valley, fate conspired to bring Robert E. Lee to command of the Army of Northern Virginia. In late May, as McClellan was forced to extend his line north to link up with troops that he expected to be sent overland to him, Johnston learned that McClellan was moving along the Chickahominy River. It was at this point that Johnston got uncharacteristically aggressive. Johnston had run out of breathing space for his army, and he believed McClellan was seeking to link up with McDowell's forces. Moreover, about a third of McClellan's army was south of the river, while the other parts of the army were still north of it, offering Johnston an enticing target. Therefore he drew up a very complex plan of attack for different wings of his army, and he struck at the Army of the Potomac at the Battle of Seven Pines on May 31, 1862.

Like McDowell's plan for First Bull Run, the plan proved too complicated for Johnston's army to execute, and after a day of bloody fighting little was accomplished from a technical standpoint. At one point during the Battle of Seven Pines, Confederates under General James Longstreet marched in the wrong direction down the wrong road, causing congestion and confusion among other Confederate units and ultimately weakening the effectiveness of the massive Confederate counterattack launched against McClellan.

The Battle of Seven Pines

From his first day in command, Lee faced a daunting, seemingly impossible challenge. McClellan had maneuvered nearly 100,000 troops to within seven miles of Richmond, three Union units were closing in on General Jackson's Confederates in Virginia's Shenandoah Valley, and a fourth Union army was camped on the Rappahannock River ostensibly ready to come to McClellan's aid. On June 12, as McClellan sat on Richmond's eastern outskirts waiting for reinforcements, Lee began to ring the city with troop entrenchments.

Although the Battle of Seven Pines was tactically inconclusive, McClellan's resolve to keep pushing forward vanished. He maneuvered his army so that it was all south of the Chickahominy, but as he settled in for an expected siege, Lee went about preparing Richmond's defenses and devising his own aggressive attacks.

With more Confederate troops swelling the ranks, Lee's army was McClellan's equal by late June, and on June 25, Lee commenced an all-out attempt to destroy McClellan's army in a series of fierce battles known as the Seven Days Battles. After a stalemate in the first fighting at Oak Grove, Lee's army kept pushing ahead, using Stonewall Jackson to attack McClellan's right. Although Stonewall Jackson was unusually lethargic during the week's fighting, the appearance of his "foot cavalry" spooked McClellan even more, and McClellan was now certain he was opposed by 200,000 men, more than double the actual size of Lee's army. It also made McClellan think that the Confederates were threatening his supply line, forcing him to shift his army toward the James River to draw supplies.

On June 26, the Union defenders sharply repulsed the Confederate attacks at Mechanicsville, in part due to the fact that Stonewall Jackson had his troops bivouac for the night despite the fact heavy gunfire indicating a large battle was popping off within earshot. When the Confederates had more success the next day at Gaines' Mills, McClellan continued his strategic retreat, maneuvering his army toward a defensive position on the James River and all but abandoning the siege.

McClellan managed to keep his forces in tact (mostly through the efforts of his field generals), ultimately retreating to Harrison's Landing on the James River and establishing a new base of operation. Feeling increasingly at odds with his superiors, in a letter sent from Gaines' Mills, Virginia dated June 28, 1862, a frustrated McClellan wrote to Secretary of War Stanton, "If I save the army now, I tell you plainly that I owe no thanks to any other person in the Washington. You have done your best to sacrifice this army." McClellan's argument, however, flies in the face of common knowledge that he had become so obsessed with having sufficient supplies that he'd actually moved to Gaines' Mill to accommodate the massive amount of provisions he'd accumulated. Ultimately unable to move his cache of supplies as quickly as his men were needed, McClellan eventually ran railroad cars full of food and supplies into the Pamunkey River rather than leave them behind for the Confederates.

Despite the fact all of Lee's battle plans had been poorly executed by his generals, particularly Stonewall Jackson, he ordered one final assault against McClellan's army at Malvern Hill. Incredibly, McClellan was not even on the field for that battle, having left via steamboat back to Harrison's Landing. Biographer Ethan Rafuse notes McClellan's absence from the battlefield was inexcusable, literally leaving the Army of the Potomac leaderless during pitched battle, but McClellan often behaved cooly under fire, so it is likely not a question of McClellan's personal courage.

Ironically, Malvern Hill was one of the Union army's biggest successes during the Peninsula Campaign. Union artillery had silenced its Confederate counterparts, but Lee still ordered an infantry attack by D.H. Hill's division, which never got within 100 yards of the Union line. After the war, Hill famously referred to Malvern Hill, "It wasn't war. It was murder." Later that evening, as General Isaac Trimble (who is best known for leading a division during Pickett's Charge at Gettysburg) began moving his troops forward as if to attack, he was stopped by Stonewall Jackson, who asked "What are you going to do?" When Trimble replied that he was going to charge, Jackson countered, "General Hill has just tried with his entire division and been repulsed. I guess you'd better not try it."

After Malvern Hill, McClellan withdrew his army to Harrison's Landing, where it was protected by the U.S. Navy along the James River and had its flanks secured by the river itself. At this point, the bureaucratic bickering between McClellan and Washington D.C. started flaring up again, as McClellan refused to recommence an advance without reinforcements. After weeks of indecision, the Army of the Potomac was finally ordered to evacuate the Peninsula and link up with John Pope's army in northern Virginia, as the Administration was more comfortable having their forces fighting on one line instead of exterior lines. Upon his arrival in Washington, McClellan told reporters that his failure to defeat Lee in Virginia was due to Lincoln not sending sufficient reinforcements.

During the Seven Days Battles, Longstreet was more effective than Jackson. In command of an entire wing of Lee's army, Longstreet aggressively attacked at Gaines' Mill and Glendale. Historians have credited Longstreet for those battles and criticized Stonewall Jackson for being unusually lethargic during the Seven Days Battles, ultimately contributing to Lee's inability to do more damage or capture McClellan's Army of the Potomac. Jackson's performance was not lost on Longstreet, who pointed out that he performed poorly at the Seven Days Battles to defend charges that Longstreet himself was slow at Gettysburg. General Lee himself called Longstreet "the staff in my right hand," and though it is now often forgotten, Longstreet became Lee's principle subordinate at this point, not Stonewall Jackson.

Similarly, Porter Alexander, the artillery chief for Longstreet's corps, was extremely critical of Stonewall Jackson's lethargy, writing in his memoirs:

"This will be even more evident in the story of Jackson's column, now to be told. His command had always before acted alone and independently. Lee's instructions to him were very brief and general, in supreme confidence that the Jackson of the Valley would win even brighter laurels on the Chickahominy. The shortest route was assigned to him and the largest force was given him. Lee then took himself off to the farthest flank, as if generously to leave to Jackson the opportunity of the most brilliant victory of the war.

His failure is not so much a military as a psychological phenomenon. He did not try and fail. He simply made no effort. The story embraces two days. He spent the 29th in camp in disregard of Lee's instructions, and he spent the 30th in equal idleness at White Oak Swamp. His 25,000 infantry practically did not fire a shot in the two days."

Jackson's performance in the Seven Days Battles has been rightly criticized, but historians are also quick to point out that his actions were likely hampered by the fatigue incurred during the Valley Campaign. Regardless, in the wake of the Seven Days Battles, Lee reorganized the Army of Northern Virginia into the structure it is best remembered by. Jackson now took command of a force consisting of his own division (now commanded by Brig. General Charles S. Winder) and those of Maj. General Richard S. Ewell, Brig. General William H. C. Whiting, and Maj. General D. H. Hill. The other wing of Lee's army was commanded by Longstreet. On July 25, 1862, after the conclusion of the Seven Days Battles had brought the Peninsula Campaign to an end, JEB Stuart was promoted to Major General and his command was upgraded to Cavalry Division, a promotion earned by his famous cavalry ride around McClellan's army earlier in the Peninsula Campaign.

As it would turn out, Jackson's Valley Campaign was only the first major campaign for the control of the strategic Shenandoah. It would be fought over for most of the rest of the war until Phil Sheridan literally put it to the torch in the final months of the war, bringing about the total war tactics the Union had started using at the beginning of 1864.

Of course, that was well into the future, and for the time being, the first and most famous Valley Campaign turned Stonewall Jackson from a respected but relatively minor general into one of the heroes of the South. He had shown fine leadership and a firm grasp of strategy and tactics. He proved to the rebel armies, who were always facing greater numbers, that a smaller force could defeat a larger one by taking advantage of separation in the enemy forces to hit smaller detachments one at a time, and achieve local superiority in numbers. Once one of the smaller detachments was defeated, an opportunity was looked for to repeat the strategy, until the entire enemy force was defeated in piecemeal fashion. This was the method of Jackson's choosing throughout the Shenandoah Valley Campaign, and the tactic is known in military circles as "defeating in detail." A staple of Napoleon's success a few generations earlier at places like Austerlitz, Civil War generals constantly sought to defeat an enemy army in detail, but these attempts were almost always in vain.

The Shenandoah Valley Campaign of 1862 was a major exception to that rule, and it is still taught in military textbooks as a classic example. As military historians Herman Hattaway and Archer Jones explained in their military history *How the North Won*, "Always outnumbered seven to three, every time Jackson engaged he fought with the odds of about four to three in his favor—because, moving rapidly on interior lines, he hit fractions of his enemy with the bulk of his own command. ... Jackson enjoyed the great advantage that the northerners remained widely scattered on a perimeter within which his troops could maneuver to concentrate against first one and then another of the Union forces. Lincoln managed very well, personally maneuvering the scattered Union armies. Since neither Lincoln nor his advisers felt that Jackson's small force could truly threaten Washington, they chose an offensive response as they sought to exploit their overwhelming forces and exterior position to overwhelm his army. But Jackson's great ability, celerity of movement, and successful series of small fights determined the outcome."

The Valley Campaign immediately made Stonewall Jackson a Southern celebrity. He was toasted in every town. Songs were written about him. At a time when the Confederacy's very existence hung in the balance, he had given the young nation victory after victory. In her diary, Confederate nurse Kate Cummings wrote, "A star has arisen: his name, the haughty foe has found, to his cost, has been given prophetically, as he proved a wall of granite to them. For four weeks he has kept at bay more than one of the boasted armies."

Jackson, however, felt ill at ease with all the attention. At the end of the Valley Campaign, he confided to his pastor, "I am afraid that our people are looking to the wrong source for help, and ascribing our success to those to whom they are not due. If we fail to Trust in God and give Him all the glory, our cause is ruined."

Chapter 4: Back at Bull Run

After the Peninsula Campaign came to a close, Lee reorganized the Army of Northern Virginia into the structure with which it is most remembered. Jackson now took command of a force consisting of his own division (now commanded by Brig. General Charles S. Winder) and those of Maj. General Richard S. Ewell, Brig. General William H. C. Whiting, and Maj. General D. H. Hill. The other wing of Lee's army was commanded by James Longstreet.

Lee and his army had pushed McClellan's Army of the Potomac away from Richmond, but there was little time for celebration in July 1862. While McClellan was trying to extricate his army from a tricky spot on the Virginian Peninsula, about 50,000 Union soldiers were menacing the Confederates in Northern Virginia, outnumbering Lee's army. If McClellan's Army of the Potomac linked up with the army now being gathered in Northern Virginia, they would vastly outnumber Lee and begin yet another drive toward Richmond. For Lee, the best option (and it was hardly a good one) was to try to prevent the two Union armies from linking up, and the only way to do that would be to inflict a decisive defeat upon the army in Northern Virginia before it was joined by McClellan's men.

Even before McClellan had completely withdrawn his troops, Lee sent Jackson northward to intercept the new army Abraham Lincoln had placed under Maj. General John Pope, formed out of the scattered troops in the Virginia area. Pope had found success in the Western theater, and he was uncommonly brash, instructing the previously defeated men now under his command that his soldiers in the West were accustomed to seeing the backs of the enemy. Pope's arrogance turned off his own men, and it also caught the notice of Lee.

Pope

On June 26, General Pope deployed his forces in an arc across Northern Virginia; its right flank under Maj. General Franz Sigel positioned at Sperryville on the Blue Ridge Mountains, its center columns under Maj. General Nathaniel P. Banks at Little Washington, and its left flank under Maj. General Irvin McDowell at Falmouth on the Rappahannock River. On July 13, Lee responded by sending Jackson with 14,000 men to Gordonsville, with Maj. General A. P. Hill's division of 10,000 men set to join him by July 27. This would set off one of the most significant battles of Jackson's military career.

On August 6, Pope marched his forces south into Culpeper County intending to capture the rail junction at Gordonsville in an attempt to draw Confederate attention away from General McClellan's withdrawal from the Virginia Peninsula. In response, Jackson went on the offensive, attacking Banks' center division, which proved precisely the right move. Jackson's larger intention was to then move on to Culpeper Court House, 26 miles north of Gordonsville-- the focal point of the Union arc--and then take on each of the Union armies separately. It was an ambitious plan to say the least.

Setting out on August 7, Jackson's march was immediately hampered by a severe heat wave, worsened by his now characteristic secrecy about his strategy. His field officers were so confused as to the exact route they were to follow that his column only progressed 8 miles over the next twenty-four hours. This slow progress allowed the Union cavalry to alert Pope of Confederate movement, and he countered by sending General Sigel to meet up with General Banks at Culpeper Court House and maintain a defensive line on a ridge above Cedar Run, seven miles to the south.

On the morning of August 9, Jackson's army crossed the Rapidan River into Culpeper County, led by Maj. General Richard S. Ewell's division, followed by Brig. General Charles S. Winder's division, with Maj. General A. P. Hill's troops picking up the rear. Just before noon, Brig. General Jubal Early's brigade, the front line of Ewell's division, came upon Union cavalry and artillery occupying the ridge above Cedar Run. Winder's division quickly formed to Early's left (on the west side of the Turnpike), with Brig. General William Taliaferro's brigade positioned closest to Early, and Col. Thomas S. Garnett's units forming on the far Confederate left. Then, Winder's artillery filled the gap on the road between the two divisions, the "Stonewall" Brigade, led by Col. Charles R. Ronald were brought up as support behind the cannons, while A. P Hill's division stood in reserve on the Confederate left. Meanwhile, the Union formed a line joining the armies of Brig. Generals Crawford, Auger, Geary, and Prince, while Brig. General George S. Greene's brigade was kept in reserve in the rear.

A little before 5:00 p.m., Confederate General Winder was mortally wounded while standing in the open attempting to direct his troops. As a result, command of his division fell to General Taliaferro, who was completely ignorant of Jackson's battle plan. Meanwhile, the Stonewall Brigade, which was supposed to come up in support, remained a half mile behind instead. Then, before leadership could be reestablished, Union forces attacked again. When Jackson's brigade finally advanced, they were quickly dispended of by Crawford's troops--with Jackson ordering the batteries withdrawn before they could be captured. At this point, Taliaferro and Early's left were hit hard by the Union advance and were nearly broken.

As the story is told, determined to inspire his men to take the offensive, Jackson suddenly rode into the battlefield and attempted to brandish his sword, but the man who had once warned his VMI cadets to be ready to throw the scabbards of their swords away found that due to the infrequency with which he had drawn it, it had rusted in its scabbard. Undaunted, he unbuckled the sword from his belt--scabbard and all--and waved it over his head. Then he grabbed a battle flag from a retreating standard bearer and called for his men to rally around him. Heartened by their commander's zeal, the Stonewall Brigade set fiercely into the Union troops, quickly driving them back. And although Union forces were subsequently able to regroup and attack, the Stonewall Brigade had given the Confederate front line time to reform and A. P Hill's troops time to come up and fill in the gaps.

Almost immediately, the Union forces collapsed and went in full retreat. Confederate infantry and General William E. Jones' 7th Virginia Cavalry chased in hot pursuit, nearly capturing Banks and Pope at their headquarters a mile behind the Union line). But with darkness setting in, Jackson decided to give up the pursuit because he was unsure of where the rest of Pope's army was positioned. For the next two days, Jackson maintained his position south of Cedar Run, waiting for a Union attack that never came. Finally, after receiving news that Pope's entire army had arrived at Culpeper Court House, on August 12, Jackson fell back to a more defensive position behind the Rapidan River.

Though steeped in difficulties and a series of errors, the Battle at Cedar Mountain was deemed an unqualified victory for the Confederacy and for Stonewall Jackson himself. He'd wreaked such havoc against the Northern forces (Union casualties numbered at over 2300) that Union General-in-Chief Henry W. Halleck called off Pope's planned advance on Gordonsville, thereby giving Lee the initiative in the Northern Virginia Campaign and effectively shifting the fighting in Virginia from the Virginia Peninsula into northern Virginia, making it essentially a Union retreat. Filling Winder's role as acting commander was Colonel William S. Baylor, who was killed three weeks later at the Second Battle of Bull Run. Following Baylor as the brigade's leader was Colonel Andrew J. Grigsby, who would lead them into Maryland and throughout the Battle of Antietam.[22]

A few weeks after Cedar Mountain, Lee sent Jackson's men stealthily past Pope's right as the two armies skirmished around the Rappahannock River from August 22-25, which preoccupied Pope and helped keep his army in place and vulnerable to Jackson's turning movement. Meanwhile, Jackson's wing of the Army of Northern Virginia was heading toward Bristoe Station and the railroad junction at Manassas, where he would be positioned not only to destroy Pope's supply lines but also potentially cut off Pope's line of retreat.

Pope learned about Jackson's turning movement on August 26, and his initial response was to try to coordinate the dispositions of the reinforcements he thought he was due to receive imminently, which would include the Black Hat Brigade. By the time Pope was aware of Jackson's move on his right, however, the Confederates were well into his rear. On the night of August 26, Jackson's men slipped through Thoroughfare Gap and headed for the railroad at Bristoe Station, cutting up the line.

By the end of August 27, Jackson's men were being chased by a Union division under the command of "Fighting Joe" Hooker, forcing Jackson to conduct a rearguard action while he retreated and dug in behind an unfinished railroad near Bull Run creek. Jackson had posted his men about a mile away from where he had become a Confederate hero the year before during First Manassas, when his brigade had rallied the Confederates on Henry Hill and turned the tide of that battle. Now he was digging in right on a spot that Union soldiers opposing him had stood on 13 months earlier.

---

[22] Cutrer, Lecture, March 9, 2011.

With the Confederate army divided and Pope's army between them, Pope was now positioned to prevent them from linking up by blocking the Thoroughfare Gap. Ultimately he opted not to, later claiming that when he saw smoke from the flames shooting near Manassas, he figured he had Jackson in trouble and could annihilate the Confederates before Longstreet reunited with them. In fact, those flames were coming from his own supplies, after Jackson's men began torching what they couldn't carry. As a result, Longstreet's wing of the army would suffer only a slight harassment from Union cavalry and one Union division before they gave way at Thoroughfare Gap.

With the path established for Longstreet's wing to march and reunite with Jackson's wing, the race was now on. Could Pope's army fall on Jackson's wing and destroy it before Longstreet rejoined it? Fittingly, the answer would be influenced heavily by Jackson and the Stonewall Brigade.

Although Pope was now planning to thrust at Jackson's army, the Second Battle of Bull Run actually began on the evening of August 28 with Jackson's men taking the offensive. Pope was in the process of gathering all his men at Centreville, just above Bull Run and a few miles away from Jackson's men, because he thought Jackson's men were at Centreville itself. Thus, as Jackson's men kept their defensive line along the unfinished railroad cut, they watched a Union column marching along the Warrenton Turnpike near Brawner's farm, and it turned out to be soldiers from Union General Rufus King's division marching toward Centreville to meet up with the rest of Pope's army and hopefully discover Jackson. Unbeknownst to the column, they were actually marching right past Jackson's entire wing of the army.

Emboldened by the news that Longstreet was passing through Thoroughfare Gap around the same time, Jackson got characteristically aggressive, and figuring that this Union column was retreating behind Bull Run to link up with Pope's army and perhaps even consisted of reinforcements from the Army of the Potomac, he decided to try to annihilate the column.

In the late afternoon, Jackson ordered his principal officers, "Bring out your men, gentlemen." With that, he ordered his artillery to open up on the column marching conspicuously across their front. As fate would have it, the part of the column in Jackson's front at this time was Gibbon's brigade of Westerners.

As the sun began to disappear behind the mountains in the west, while his men were focused on reaching Centreville overnight, Union General John Gibbon, the leader of a unit that would soon become known as the Iron Brigade, suddenly caught sight of what looked like several horsemen at the Brawner farmhouse in the distance. After turning off the pike to take a better look, Gibbon quickly realized that the men were not cavalry, but Confederate artillery, who seemed to be preparing to attack. Before he could warn his men, two Confederate batteries opened fire on the western brigade, scattering the column and sending ambulances and wagons careening off the road in panic.

Gibbon immediately called up Battery B of the 4th U.S. Artillery to assume battle positions just east of the Brawner farmhouse. Union and Confederate gunners exchanged fire, the ground shaking and the air booming with each round. Jackson pulled his gunners back and sent in another battery on Gibbon's left, just as he was ordering the brigade off the road and into the cover of forest on the opposite side of the Brawner farm.

John Hatch's brigade of King's division had already marched past Jackson's front, so Gibbon worked to get reinforcements from Abner Doubleday's brigade and formed a battle line. Due to Pope's belief that Jackson was at Centreville, Gibbon mistakenly thought that the artillery being fired at them was coming from JEB Stuart's cavalry, and that two brigades could sweep them aside and end the harassment of their march. The men of the Iron Brigade had never fought before, and now they were about to make a general advance against half of the Army of Northern Virginia.

Underestimating the size of Jackson's entire force, Gibbon deployed the 2nd Wisconsin to handle what seemed like just a few batteries. He instructed the 2nd Wisconsin to advance through woods on the Confederates' right flank. In fact, when Gibbon convened with the regiment in the woods, he instructed them to capture the artillery, but in reality, he was posting a lone regiment on the right flank of Richard S. Ewell's entire division, which was supported in the rear by William Taliaferro's division.

With his line formed, Gibbon's previously untested men began moving forward, only to come face to face with Confederates at nearly point blank range in Brawner's farm. Major Rufus Dawes, who would become a hero on Day 1 at Gettysburg in command of the 6th Wisconsin, described the fighting the 6th Wisconsin endured that night, "Our men on the left loaded and fired with the energy of madmen, and the 6th worked with equal desperation. This stopped the rush of the enemy and they halted and fired upon us their deadly musketry. During a few awful moments, I could see by the lurid light of the powder flashes, the whole of both lines. The two ... were within ... fifty yards of each other pouring musketry into each other as fast as men could load and shoot."

Meanwhile, the 2nd Wisconsin came through the woods and found themselves squarely on the Confederates' right flank at an angle that also happened to expose their own right flank. Thankfully for the Union, the 2nd Wisconsin was one of the few veteran regiments on the field that night, and they stood firm even after the Stonewall Brigade unleashed the first volley, firing a volley of their own and thus starting a general musketry exchange. Out of the nearly 430 men fighting for the 2nd Wisconsin, nearly 60% were about to become casualties.

The fact that daylight was running out likely contributed to the confusion that induced Gibbon to stand firm against the artillery assault, but it would also prove to be his saving grace. Gibbon shored up the right of his line with men from Doubleday's brigade and kept plugging in gaps in his line, and the fighting was so hot that Jackson actually started personally directing regiments into the fighting. However, while Jackson was ordering multiple regiments into the fray, the unwitting Gibbon was countering by ordering up single regiments. Jackson described the fighting, "In a few moments our entire line was engaged in a fierce and sanguinary struggle with the enemy. As one line was repulsed another took its place and pressed forward as if determined by force of numbers and fury of assault to drive us from our positions."

The Federals and Confederates fired back and forth, frozen in their positions for nearly half an hour before Confederate reinforcements widened the line against the 2nd Wisconsin. Brigadier General Gibbon immediately dispatched over 400 of the 19th Indiana to bolster the 2nd Wisconsin's left flank and hold the line. As night approached, Jackson enlisted the help of Brigadier General Alexander Lawton's four Georgia regiments, and led them against the 2nd Wisconsin's right flank. Gibbon sent the 7th Wisconsin to meet them, but once again the Westerners found themselves outnumbered more than two to one.

The two sides continued to bombard one another with rifle fire as the night wore on. Even though the Confederate soldiers far outnumbered the Iron Brigade, the latter fought with what Jackson called such "obstinate determination" that he became increasingly and uncharacteristically desperate, calling on more and more troops to contain and defeat the Federal brigade.[23] Just before Jackson dispatched Isaac Trimble's 1,200-man brigade to reinforce the Stonewall Brigade's left, Gibbon had sent the 6th Wisconsin to lengthen his wall of troops on the right side. The 6th Wisconsin bombarded Trimble's troops with such force that they were forced to a halt just as the Stonewall Brigade had been earlier in the day.

The regiments of the Black Hat Brigade were proving themselves in this unfair matchup, but were losing the manpower to continue such a brave stand. Gibbon called for nearby reinforcements, but no one came. Finally, General Abner Doubleday independently sent the 76th New York and 56th Pennsylvania from his brigade to aid Gibbon's men, closing the gap between the 7th and 6th Wisconsin and reinforcing Gibbon's dwindling line. With this addition, Gibbon's numbers were catching up to Jackson's 3,000, and Jackson began to buckle under pressure. He ordered the rest of the troops in reserve on the offensive, but several had already bivouacked for the night and only a couple of regiments responded, and many of them stumbled or were injured moving down the hillside in the dark. In the meantime, the 6th Wisconsin and 56th Pennsylvania had teamed up to overpower Jackson's attacking line, in what became a bloody mistake for the Confederates.

Nevertheless, Jackson determinedly turned to General Lawton's brigade to continue his forward drive, and was once again thwarted by the Badgers and their comrades. The 7th Wisconsin and the 76th New York swung their positions to the south, crushing Lawton's flank of Georgians and stopping them in their tracks. As every move Jackson made was met with an iron response on the part of Gibbon's brigade, the battle deteriorated into a stalemate. Both sides

[23] Thompson, "A Legend is Born at Brawner's Farm."

continued firing at one another in the darkness, fighting for over three hours less than 30 yards apart. Finally, the Confederates, and soon after the Federals, ran out of motivation and ammunition, and began to focus on evacuating their wounded from the battlefield.[24]

By 9:00, the Union soldiers fought a gradual retreat back to the turnpike, leaving the field to Jackson's men. As the first fighting of what would become the Second Battle of Bull Run came to a close, both sides came to terms with the heavy losses suffered during the night. Gibbon's brigade lost nearly 800 killed or wounded, while the Stonewall Brigade had lost 340 men. The fighting had been so intense that nearly one in every three men had been hit at least once. Furthermore, the Confederate casualties included Ewell and Taliaferro, two of Jackson's division commanders.

The mostly inexperienced Union soldiers had held their own against the famous Stonewall Brigade, demonstrating its iron resolve in the face of a larger, more experienced army. As fate would have it, the Iron Brigade and Stonewall Brigade would face off several more times in the coming weeks.

While Jackson had repositioned his men on the defense, waiting for Longstreet to join him, Pope had determined that Jackson was retreating, and sent only a few brigades to flank and capture him. Longstreet and his 25,000 troops soon appeared, assisting Jackson's defense and turning the Confederate strategy to the offensive, catching Pope completely off-guard.

Chapter 5: Back at Harper's Ferry

After the Second Battle of Bull Run, Lee had achieved another major victory, and he now stood unopposed in the field 12 miles away from Washington D.C. While Joseph Johnston and P.G.T. Beauregard had stayed in this position in the months after the First Battle of Bull Run, Lee determined upon a more aggressive course: taking the fight to the North.

In early September, convinced that the best way to defend Richmond was to divert attention to Washington, Lee had decided to invade Maryland after obtaining Jefferson Davis's permission. Today the decision to invade Maryland is remembered through the prism of Lee hoping to win a major battle in the North that would bring about European recognition of the Confederacy, potential intervention, and possible capitulation by the North, whose anti-war Democrats were picking up political momentum. However, Lee also hoped that the fighting in Maryland would relieve Virginia's resources, especially the Shenandoah Valley, which served as the state's "breadbasket". And though largely forgotten today, Lee's move was controversial among his own men. Confederate soldiers, including Lee, took up arms to defend their homes, but now they were being asked to invade a Northern state. An untold number of Confederate soldiers refused to cross the Potomac River into Maryland.

---

[24] Nolan, *The Iron Brigade*, 87-96; Thompson, "A Legend is Born at Brawner's Farm"

Lee had also no doubt taken stock of the North's morale, both among its people and the soldiers of Pope's army and McClellan's army. In the summer of 1862, the Union had suffered more than 20,000 casualties, and Northern Democrats, who had been split into pro-war and anti-war factions from the beginning, increasingly began to question the war. As of September 1862, no progress had been made on Richmond; in fact, a Confederate army was now about to enter Maryland. And with the election of 1862 was approaching, Lincoln feared the Republicans might suffer losses in the Congressional midterms that would harm the war effort.

With all of that in mind, he restored General McClellan and removed General Pope after the second disaster at Bull Run. McClellan was still immensely popular among the Army of the Potomac, and with a mixture of men from his Army of the Potomac and Pope's Army of Virginia, he began a cautious pursuit of Lee into Maryland.

Although McClellan had largely stayed out of the political fray through 1862, McClellan's most ardent supporters could not deny that he actively worked to delay reinforcing Pope during the Second Manassas campaign once the Army of the Potomac was evacuated from the Peninsula. Nevertheless, McClellan ultimately got what he wanted out of Pope's misfortune. Though there is some debate on the order of events that led to McClellan taking command, Lincoln ultimately restored McClellan to command, likely because McClellan was the only administrator who could reform the army quickly and efficiently.

McClellan

Naturally, McClellan's ascension to command of the armies around Washington outraged the Republicans in Congress and the Lincoln Administration, some of whom had all but branded him a traitor for his inactivity in early 1862 and his poor performance on the Peninsula. This would make it all the more ironic that McClellan's campaign into Maryland during the next few weeks would bring about the release of the Emancipation Proclamation.

The most fateful decision of the Maryland Campaign was made almost immediately, when early on Lee decided to divide his army into four parts across Maryland. Lee ordered Longstreet's men to Boonsboro and then to Hagerstown, Stonewall Jackson's forces to Harpers Ferry, and Stuart's cavalry and D.H. Hill's division to screen the Army of Northern Virginia's movements and cover its rear.

Why Lee chose to divide his army is still heavily debated among historians, who have pointed to factors like the importance of maintaining his supply lines through the Shenandoah Valley. Lee was also unaware what kind of resistance he might face at places like Frederick and Harpers Ferry, and it's also possible that he simply assumed McClellan's caution would allow him to take and keep the initiative and dictate the course of the campaign. With McClellan now assuming command of the Northern forces, Lee probably expected to have plenty of time to assemble his troops and bring his battle plan to fruition.

This time, however, McClellan was better prepared to face Lee. He had beaten Lee in a campaign through western Virginia in 1861 and had clearly underestimated Lee as a result during the Peninsula Campaign, but now he realized that Lee was not the timid, indecisive general McClellan initially thought.

Though it was clear in early September that Lee had crossed the Potomac, the Army of Northern Virginia decided to use ridges, mountains and cavalry to screen their movements. McClellan believed the most realistic goal was to drive the Confederates out of Maryland and aimed to do so, but his 85,000 strong Army of the Potomac moved conservatively into Maryland during the early portion of the campaign while still dealing with logistics. A report from the infamous intelligence chief Allan Pleasanton reached McClellan and estimated the Rebel force at 100,000, while other reports couldn't ascertain the nature of the that army's movements or motives. McClellan told the Administration on September 10 that the estimates of the Army of Northern Virginia put it somewhere between 80,000-150,000 men, which obviously had a huge effect on the campaign.

With the benefit of hindsight, historians now believe that Lee's entire Army of Northern Virginia had perhaps 50,000 men at most and possibly closer to 30,000 during the Maryland campaign. It's unclear how Lee's army, which numbered 55,000 before the Maryland Campaign, suffered such a steep drop in manpower, but historians have cited a number of factors, including disease and soldiers' refusal to invade the North.

On September 12, Stonewall Jackson's men were making their way to the outskirts of Harpers Ferry, whose garrison McClellan had unsuccessfully requested to have evacuated and added to his army. Meanwhile, the Union army was on the verge of entering Frederick, still unaware of Lee's dispositions but less than 20 miles behind the fragmented Confederate army.

It was around Frederick that the North was about to have one of the greatest strokes of luck during the Civil War. For reasons that are still unclear, Union troops in camp at Frederick came across a copy of Special Order 191, wrapped up among three cigars. The order contained Lee's entire marching plans for Maryland, making it clear that the Army of Northern Virginia had been divided into multiple parts, which, if faced by overpowering strength, could be entirely defeated in detail and bagged separately before they could regather into one fighting force.

The "Lost Order" quickly made its way to General McClellan, who took several hours to debate whether or not it was intentional misinformation or actually real. McClellan is usually faulted for not acting quickly enough on these orders, but much of the instructions are vague and seemingly contradicted recent Rebel movements. Moreover, McClellan was rightly concerned that the orders could be false misinformation meant to deceive the Union, since the manner in which the orders were lost was bizarre and could not be accounted for. After about 18 hours,

McClellan was confident enough that they were accurate and famously boasted to General Gibbon, "Here is a paper with which if I cannot whip Bobby Lee, I will be willing to go home." McClellan also wired Lincoln, "I have the whole rebel force in front of me, but I am confident, and no time shall be lost. I think Lee has made a gross mistake, and that he will be severely punished for it. I have all the plans of the rebels, and will catch them in their own trap if my men are equal to the emergency... Will send you trophies."

Though having Lee's marching plans offered McClellan an incredible advantage, the Lost Order may also have reinforced McClellan's belief that Lee's army had a significant advantage in manpower through its vague wording of "commands."

Harpers Ferry in the 1860s

As General Lee marched his Army of Northern Virginia down the Shenandoah Valley into Maryland, he planned to capture the garrison and arsenal at Harpers Ferry to secure his supply line back to Virginia. But even before they were far into Maryland, Jackson and A.P. Hill were getting on each other's nerves, and after one scolding from Jackson on September 3, witnesses noticed Hill responded to the reprimand "rather sullenly, his face flushing up."

During another march, Hill became furious after finding that Jackson had directly ordered his division to halt without informing Hill of the change in plans. When Hill asked his subordinates why they halted, and he was informed that it was Jackson's orders, he confronted Jackson and offered him his sword, telling him, "If you take command of my troops in my presence, take my sword also." Jackson responded, "Put up your sword and consider yourself in arrest." Another Confederate soldier remembered afterward that Hill "marched on foot with the rear guard all the day through Maryland, an old white hat slouched over his eyes, his coat off and wearing an old flannel shirt, looking mad as a bull."

Eventually, both of the generals cooled their tempers, and by September 10 Hill was asking to be restored to command ahead of battle, a request Jackson granted. A Confederate noted that after being restored to command, Hill " mounted his horse and dashed to the front of his troops, and looking like a young eagle in search of his prey, took command of his division to the delight of all his men."

The Confederates were completely unaware of the Army of the Potomac's luck as they began to carry out Lee's plans, and Stonewall Jackson was already in the process of forcing the capitulation of Harpers Ferry.

To Stonewall Jackson's advantage, Col. Dixon S. Miles, Union commander at Harpers Ferry, had insisted on keeping most of his troops near the town instead of taking up commanding positions on the most important position, Maryland Heights. On September 12, Confederate forces engaged the Union's marginal defenses on the heights, but only a brief skirmish ensued. Then on September 13, two Confederate brigades arrived and easily drove the Union troops from the heights, even as critical positions to the west and south of town remained heavily defended.

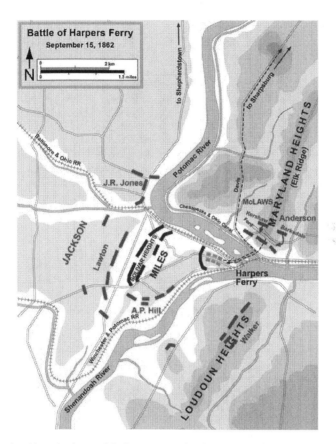

On September 14, as the Army of the Potomac was bearing down on the Confederates around South Mountain several miles away, Jackson had methodically positioned his artillery around Harpers Ferry and ordered Maj. Gen. A. P. Hill to move down the west bank of the Shenandoah River in preparation for a flank attack on the Union left the next morning. While Miles suggested surrendering, several officers among the garrison argued that they should attempt a breakout. When Miles suggested it was a "wild and impractical" idea, Benjamin "Grimes" Davis made clear that he would attempt it with men from the 12th Illinois Cavalry, the Loudoun Rangers, and other small units. Eventually, Davis successfully led about 1,400 out of Harpers Ferry and inadvertently ran into the wagon train carrying Longstreet's ordnance. Porter Alexander, the chief artillerist of Longstreet's corps, explained, "My reserve ordnance train, of about 80 wagons, had accompanied Lee's headquarters to Hagerstown, and had also followed the march back to Boonsboro. I was now ordered to cross the Potomac at Williamsport, and go thence to Shepherdstown, where I should leave the train and come in person to Sharpsburg. The moon was rising as I started, and about daylight I forded the Potomac, unaware of having had a narrow escape from capture, with my train, by Gregg's brigade of cavalry. This brigade had escaped that night from Harper's Ferry, and crossed our line of retreat from Boonsboro. It had captured and destroyed the reserve ordnance train, of 45 wagons of Longstreet's corps."

By the following morning, September 15, Jackson had positioned nearly fifty guns on Maryland Heights and at the base of Loudoun Heights. Then he began a fierce artillery barrage from all sides, followed by a full-out infantry assault. Realizing the hopelessness of the situation, Col. Miles raised the white flag of surrender, enraging some of the men, one of whom beseeched him, "Colonel, don't surrender us. Don't you hear the signal guns? Our forces are near us. Let us cut our way out and join them." Miles dismissed the suggestion, insisting, "They will blow us out of this place in half an hour." Almost on cue, an exploding artillery shell mortally wounded Miles, and some historians have argued Miles was fragged by Union soldiers.

Jackson had lost less than 300 casualties while forcing the surrender of nearly 12,500 Union soldiers at Harpers Ferry, the largest number of Union soldiers to surrender at once during the entire war. For the rest of the day, the Confederates helped themselves to supplies in the garrison, including food, uniforms, and more, as Jackson sent a letter to Lee informing him of the success, "Through God's blessing, Harper's Ferry and its garrison are to be surrendered." Already a legend, Jackson earned the attention of the surrendered Union troops, who tried to catch a glimpse of him only to be surprised at his rather disheveled look. One of the men remarked, "Boys, he isn't much for looks, but if we'd had him we wouldn't have been caught in this trap."

Jackson had little time to celebrate before hearing back from Lee ordering him to quickly march to Sharpsburg as soon as he could. But the surrender of Harpers Ferry still needed to be fully processed, so Jackson ordered A.P. Hill's Light Division to remain at Harpers Ferry and carry out all the necessities, including the parole of the Union prisoners. Jackson would recount in his post-battle report, "By a severe night's march we reached the vicinity of Sharpsburg on the morning of the 16th."

Chapter 6: Antietam

It's unclear when Lee realized that McClellan had found a copy of his marching orders, and it's even possible that he knew almost right away. But that still gave Lee, who only had about 18,000 men at his disposal in the vicinity, little time to regroup. On the night of September 13 McClellan's army began moving at an uncharacteristically quick pace, and the following day, the advancing Union army began pushing in on the Confederate forces at several mountain passes at South Mountain: Crampton's Gap, Turner's Gap, and Fox's Gap. If McClellan's men could successfully push their way through these gaps, they would have an even greater chance of falling upon the different pieces of Lee's army.

While the victory at South Mountain boosted the morale of the Union army, the strategic defeat of the Confederates in that battle prompted Lee to reconsider his Maryland campaign. At the same time, McClellan's inaction in the wake of Lee's retreat, and the victory of Jackson's forces at Harper's Ferry on September 15, gave Lee both time and resolve to set up a strong defense at Sharpsburg, along Antietam Creek.

McClellan's lead elements arrived around Sharpsburg on the night of September 15, and the rest of the army came up on September 16, but McClellan did not order a general attack that day out of fear that he was still heavily outnumbered. Had he done so, he would not only have had an overwhelming advantage but would not have had to deal with A.P. Hill's Light Division, which was still busy at Harper's Ferry. The rest of Stonewall Jackson's men made it to Sharpsburg ahead of the climactic battle the next day.

By the time the Federal soldiers bivouacked along the Hagerstown Turnpike just northwest of Antietam Creek, the Confederate line had stretched three and a half miles, running in a north-south direction along the divide between Antietam Creek and the Potomac. With McClellan's men all in position on the night of the 16th, McClellan decided to give general battle on the 17th. Longstreet described the scene before the battle commenced: "The blue uniforms of the federals appeared among the trees that crowned the heights on the eastern bank of the Antietam. The number increased, and larger and larger grew the field of blue until is seemed to stretch as far as the eye could see, and from the tops of the mountains down to the edge of the stream gathered the great army of McClellan."[25]

Still operating under the belief that he was outnumbered, McClellan's plan was to break Lee's left flank in the northern sector, because the crosses that he knew about over Antietam Creek (Burnside's Bridge and the bridge leading to Boonsboro) were held on the other side by Confederates who could operate along the high ground. McClellan's cavalry had not scouted other passes along Antietam Creek, and he and his officers seemed to be unaware that the Antietam Creek was so shallow in places around those bridges that the men could have waded across without trying to squeeze across bridges.

Worried about being outnumbered, McClellan's plan called for an assault with only half his army, starting with two corps along the Confederate left, and the support of perhaps a third or fourth corps. Meanwhile, he initially planned to launch diversionary attacks in the center and the Confederate right. However, the late night skirmishing and probing conducted by men of Hooker's I Corps on the night of the 16th suggested to Lee that they would attack there in force on the morning of the 17th, and before the battle he bolstered his left flank. He also sent word to A.P. Hill and Lafayette McLaws to force march with all haste to Sharpsburg.

[25]   Gaffney, P., and D. Gaffney. *The Civil War: Exploring History One Week at a Time.* Page 179.

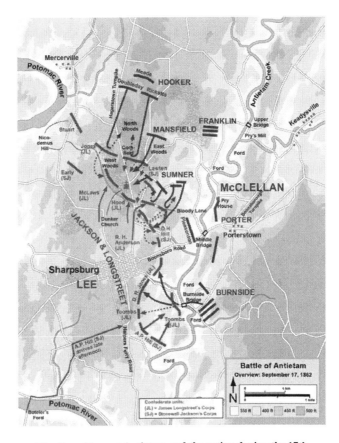

The dispositions at Antietam and the action during the 17th

As luck would have it, the early part of the fighting at Antietam would pit the Stonewall Brigade against the Iron Brigade once again. As Lee had guessed, and as McClellan intended, the Battle of Antietam began near dawn on the morning of the 17th, with the advance of Hooker's I Corps down the Hagerstown Turnpike toward the small white Dunker Church, a small one room building that served as a church for a small group of German Baptists. Initially opposing Hooker's 8,500 man Corps were Stonewall Jackson's men, which numbered just under 8,000. Jackson's defenders were deployed across the Turnpike in the West Woods on the left, and a cornfield on the right.

The Dunker Church in the background

Hooker decided to start the fighting with an artillery bombardment due to the fact that the nature of the terrain made it unclear what his corps would be facing in the cornfield and the West Woods. Hooker's men could see the Confederates' bayonets shining in the cornfield, but the corn was high enough to conceal their number. During the artillery duel, infantry pushed forward until there was a fierce pitched battle in the cornfield, including hand-to-hand fighting. Colonel Benjamin Cook of the 12th Massachusetts later recalled his experience in the cornfield as "the most deadly fire of the war. Rifles are shot to pieces in the hands of the soldiers, canteens and haversacks are riddled with bullets, the dead and wounded go down in scores."

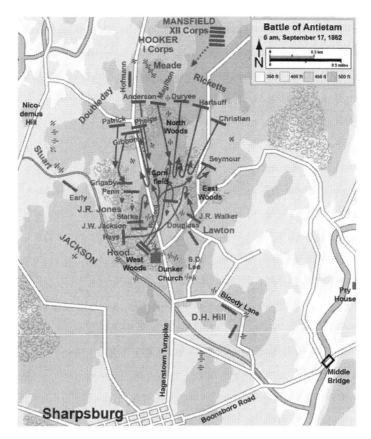

The fighting was fierce, remembered Major Rufus Dawes of the 6th Wisconsin (the Iron Brigade), who stated, "'Men, I cannot say fell; they were knocked out of the ranks by dozens...There was, on the part of the men, great hysterical excitement, eagerness to go forward, and a reckless disregard of life, of everything but victory."[26]

After falling back from the Cornfield, the Stonewall Brigade took cover in the West Woods behind brush and rocks, sniping away at Yankee soldiers at every opportunity. The West Woods, Cornfield, and Dunker Church were quickly covered with the dead and wounded. McClellan ordered his men on his right (the Confederate left) to fall back, not realizing that only one further surge was necessary to compress the entire left Confederate flank.

---

[26] McPherson, *Antietam*, 117.

Although McClellan had dispatched his troops piecemeal into the fight, the Union army had dealt heavy blows to the Confederate troops and gained substantial ground that morning. Despite Jackson's valiant defense, the Union advance kept pushing forward along the West Woods and the Turnpike, and Jackson's line was on the verge of collapse by 7:00 a.m. In one of the most legendary parts of the battle, John Bell Hood's Texans had come up to the field and had not eaten breakfast, so they were held in reserve and allowed to start preparing a meal. Just before they could eat, however, they were called into action, infuriating his men. Thankfully for the Confederates, it would be the Union who felt the brunt of their fury.

Hood

Hood's brigade drove eastward, pushing against the exhausted Federal line, and the colors of the Iron Brigade fell as the exhausted 2nd and 6th Wisconsin began to retreat into the cornfield, when Gibbon himself stopped to rally the troops. Gibbon picked up the colors, and waving the regimental flag, urged the troops to remain stalwart and return enemy fire. Witnessing the new Confederate advance on their brothers, the 7th Wisconsin and 19th Indiana crossed the turnpike and assaulted the Confederate flank with such intensity that the Southerners began to flee. The 7th and 19th chased the Confederates back through the cornfield, until the Federals stumbled and once again retreated eastward, running from the Confederates. The battle continued to be a disorganized mess of firing back and forth between the Federals and Confederates in what Hood described as "the most terrible clash of arms, by far, that has occurred during the war."[27]

Jackson discussed his men's fighting in his post-battle report:

"About sunrise the Federal infantry advanced in heavy force to the edge of the wood on the eastern side of the turnpike, driving in our skirmishers. Batteries were opened in front from the the wood with shell and canister, and our troops became exposed for near an hour to a terrific storm of shell, canister, and musketry. Gen. Jones having been compelled to leave the field, the command of Jackson's division devolved upon Gen. Starke. With heroic spirit our lines advanced to the conflict, and maintained their position, in the face of superior numbers, with stubborn resolution, sometimes driving the enemy before them and sometimes compelled to fall back before their well-sustained and destructive fire. Fresh troops from time to time relieved the enemy's ranks, and the carnage on both sides was terrific.

At this early hour Gen. Starke was killed. Col. Douglass, commanding Lawton's brigade, was also killed. Gen. Lawton, commanding division, and Col. Walker, commanding brigade, were severely wounded. More than half of the brigades of Lawton and Hays were either killed or wounded, and more than a third of Trimble's, and all the regimental commanders in those brigades, except two, were killed or wounded. Thinned in their ranks and exhausted of their ammunition, Jackson's division and the brigades of Lawton, Hays, and Trimble retired to the rear, and Hood, of Longstreet's command, again took the position from which he had been before relieved.

In the mean time Gen. Stuart moved his artillery to a position nearer to the main command, and more in our rear. Early, being now directed, in consequence of the disability of Gen. Lawton, to take command of Ewell's division, returned with his brigade (with the exception of the Thirteenth Virginia Regiment, which remained with Gen. Stuart) to the piece of wood where he had left the other brigades of his division when he was separated from them. Here he found that the enemy had advanced his infantry near the wood in which was the Dunkard church, and had planted a battery across the turnpike near the edge of the wood and an open field, and that the brigades of Lawton, Hays, and Trimble had fallen back some distance to the rear. Finding here Cols. Grigsby and Stafford, with a portion of Jackson's division, which formed on his left, he determined to maintain his position there if re-enforcements could be sent to his support, of which he was promptly assured. Col. Grigsby, with his small command, kept in check the advance of the enemy on the left flank, while Gen. Early attacked with great vigor and gallantry the column on his right and front."

[27] Nolan, *The Iron Brigade*, 140-141.

The cornfield at Antietam. Joe Hooker reported that "every stalk of corn in the northern and greater part of the field was cut as closely as could have been done with a knife, and the slain lay in rows precisely as they had stood in their ranks a few moments before."

Dead soldiers along the turnpike at Antietam. Antietam was the first battle in which war dead were photographed and made publicly available, stunning Americans.

The struggle in the cornfield continued until further Confederate reinforcements—Jubal Early's brigade and Stuart's gunners—shifted the battle further east. Hood's division had helped the Confederates stave off the first major assault in the West Woods, and Hooker's attack fizzled out in part because Hooker was seriously injured during the fighting. Hooker had been seemingly everywhere during the fighting, and many of his comrades believed that Antietam would have turned out differently had he not been injured. Hooker was replaced by George Meade, who would ironically also replace Hooker as commander of the Army of the Potomac just before the Battle of Gettysburg.

By the end of the afternoon, Union attacks on the flanks and the center of the line had been violent but eventually unsuccessful. Aware that his army was badly bloodied but fearing Lee had many more men than he did, McClellan refused to commit fresh reserves from Franklin's VI Corps or Fitz-John Porter's V Corps. McClellan's decision was probably sealed by Fitz John Porter telling him, "Remember, General, I command the last reserve of the last Army of the Republic." Thus, the day ended in a tactical stalemate, with the Union suffering nearly 12,500 casualties (including over 2,000 dead) and the Confederates suffering over 10,000 casualties (including over 1,500 dead). Nearly 1/4th of the Army of the Potomac had been injured, captured or killed, and the same could be said for nearly 1/3rd of Lee's Army of Northern Virginia. It was the deadliest and bloodiest day in American history.

On the morning of September 18, Lee's army prepared to defend against a Union assault that ultimately never came. Finally, an improvised truce was declared to allow both sides to exchange their wounded. That evening, Lee's forces began withdrawing across the Potomac to return to Virginia.

McClellan made one push against Lee's army at nearby Shepherdstown. Shortly before dusk on September 19, Union Brig. General Charles Griffin sent 2,000 infantry and sharpshooters from Maj. General Fitz-John Porter's V Corps across the Potomac River at Boteler's Ford (also known as Shepardstown Ford) in pursuit, only to pull them back the following day when Stonewall Jackson's men entered the fray. However, Union General Adelbert Ames had mistakenly received orders to advance across the Potomac into Virginia, so he sent the 20th Maine regiment wading into the water, which actually encountered retreating Union troops as they did, and they were promptly fired upon by a barrage of Confederate artillery.

As the Battle of Shepherdstown indicated, Lee's rear guard was formidable enough that officers throughout the Army of the Potomac concurred with McClellan's actions not to go after the Army of Northern Virginia. Lee's army then moved toward the Shenandoah Valley while the Army of the Potomac hovered around Sharpsburg.

Although Antietam ended as a tactical draw, the Maryland Campaign is now widely considered a turning point in the Civil War. It resulted in forcing Lee's army out of Maryland and back into Virginia, making it a strategic victory for the North and an opportune time for President Abraham Lincoln to issue the Emancipation Proclamation. James McPherson would summarize the critical importance of the Maryland Campaign: "No other campaign and battle in the war had such momentous, multiple consequences as Antietam. In July 1863 the dual Union triumphs at Gettysburg and Vicksburg struck another blow that blunted a renewed Confederate offensive in the East and cut off the western third of the Confederacy from the rest. In September 1864 Sherman's capture of Atlanta reversed another decline in Northern morale and set the stage for the final drive to Union victory. These also were pivotal moments. But they would never have happened if the triple Confederate offensives in Mississippi, Kentucky, and most of all Maryland had not been defeated in the fall of 1862."

Chapter 7: Fredericksburg

Despite heavily outnumbering the Southern army and badly damaging it during the battle of Antietam, McClellan decided not to pursue Lee across the Potomac, citing shortages of equipment and the fear of overextending his forces. General-in-Chief Henry W. Halleck wrote in his official report, "The long inactivity of so large an army in the face of a defeated foe, and during the most favorable season for rapid movements and a vigorous campaign, was a matter of great disappointment and regret." Lincoln had also had enough of McClellan's constant excuses for not taking forward action, and he relieved McClellan of his command of the Army of the Potomac on November 7, effectively ending the general's military career.

In place of McClellan, Lincoln appointed Burnside, who had just failed at Antietam. Burnside didn't believe he was competent to command the entire army, a very honest (and accurate) judgment. However, Burnside also didn't want the command to fall upon Joe Hooker, who had been injured while aggressively fighting with his I Corps at Antietam in the morning. Thus, he accepted.

Burnside

Under pressure from Lincoln to be aggressive, Burnside laid out a difficult plan to cross the Rappahannock and attack the Confederates near Fredericksburg. The plan was doomed from the very beginning. On December 12, Burnside's army struggled to cross the river under fire from Confederate sharpshooters in the town.

The battle is mostly remembered however for the piecemeal attacks the Union army made on heavily fortified positions Longstreet's men took up on Marye's Heights. The Northern soldiers were mowed down again and again. As men lay dying on the field that night, the Northern Lights made a rare appearance. Southern soldiers took it as a divine omen and wrote about it frequently in their diaries. The Union soldiers saw less divine inspiration in the Northern Lights and mentioned it less in their own. The Battle of Fredericksburg also spawned one of Lee's most memorable quotes. During the battle, Lee turned to Longstreet and commented, "It is well that war is so terrible, otherwise we would grow too fond of it."[28]

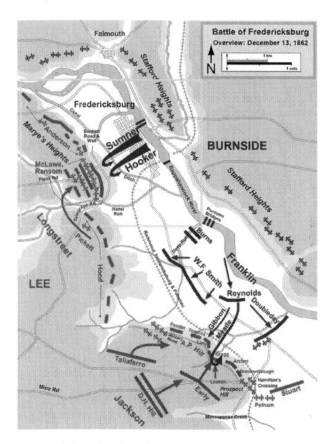

What's often forgotten is how close the Union came to dislodging Stonewall Jackson's men on the right. On the morning of December 13, a dense fog hung in the valley Fredericksburg is located in, keeping the armies hidden from each other, and while the armies bided their time Grand Division Commander William Franklin instructed I Corps commander John Reynolds to choose one of his divisions to make an attack in Stonewall Jackson's sector, and Reynolds tapped George Meade's 4,500 man division, to be supported by John Gibbon's division. Abner Doubleday's division was to cover the advance's left flank by facing south and combating JEB Stuart's cavalry, which had situated itself at a nearly 90 degree angle on the Confederates' right flank to offer enfilading fire.

28   Nagel, Paul C. *The Lee's of Virginia.* Page 179.

Meade's men began their advance forward in heavy fog around 8:30 a.m. with Gibbon's division in back of them, and as they reached Richmond Road, they began receiving enfilading fire from JEB Stuart's artillery, being manned by the young "gallant" Major John Pelham, who opened on them with 2 guns. As Union artillery tried to silence Pelham's guns from their dangerous position, Stuart told Pelham he could withdraw, to which Pelham responded, "Tell the General I can hold my ground." The 24th Michigan Infantry, a brand new regiment full of raw recruits, was ordered to deal with Pelham, but they were unable to stop Pelham's battery until it began to run low on ammunition after about an hour. Lee would later praise the young Major, stating, "It is glorious to see such courage in one so young."

"Gallant John Pelham"

Once the fog started to lift around 10:30, Jackson's artillery began raining down on the advancing Union soldiers from Prospect Hill, stopping Meade's division in its tracks about 600 yards from the hill around 11:00 a.m. As Meade's men stayed in place under heavy fire from Jackson's corps on Prospect Hill, Meade got ever more desperate about finding someone, anyone, to support his division in the attack.

Despite the fact Jackson's men had been in the area for two weeks, Jackson's line had only been formed the day before when all of his divisions were recalled from the various crossing points downriver of Fredericksburg. When they formed a line, A.P. Hill's Light Division had a 600 yard gap in it near a small, swampy patch of woods. If the Confederates thought Union men would not hit the gap, they were unpleasantly surprised when Meade's 1st brigade poured into the gap and hit one of the brigades in A.P. Hill's division right on its flank. Confederate brigadier

Maxcy Gregg was so taken by surprise that he initially thought Meade's men were Confederate comrades and ordered his men not to fire. When he rode to the front of his own line, his mistake cost him his life when one of the advancing Union soldiers shot him through the spine.

Fortunately for the Confederates, they were able to plug their gap by sending forth Jubal Early's division and William Taliaferro's division at just the right time. Meanwhile, as Meade's men fought desperately to exploit the Confederate mistake and keep a gap open, officers in the rear vacillated over how to proceed. Gibbon refused to let any of his brigades support Meade's assault, operating under the belief that he was supposed to maintain a support position. One of his brigades would not move forward to Meade's help until 1:30 p.m., more than 2 hours after Meade's men had started the assault. 2 more brigades followed, but all three of these were sharply repulsed. Yet another supporting brigade was thrown into the fray, but the Confederates drove them back in fierce hand-to-hand fighting that drove the disorganized Union soldiers back. Simply put, the supporting brigades had made their attacks too late to help Meade's breakthrough in Jackson's line. An enraged Meade complained to his corps commander, "My God, General Reynolds, did they think my division could whip Lee's whole army?"

Chapter 8: Chancellorsville

Shortly before the battle of Fredericksburg, Jackson learned that he had become a father, receiving a letter informing him of the birth of his daughter, Julia Laura Jackson, on November 23. Also before the battle, renowned cavalry chief J.E.B. Stuart gave Jackson a new outfit to replace the battle worn coat Jackson had been using throughout the war. However, Jackson ultimately refused to wear it for the next few months, his shyness once again surfacing. Ultimately, he took his last picture in it for a portrait on April 26, 1863, less than a week before the Battle of Chancellorsville.

Jackson's final photo

Lee and Jackson had just concluded an incredibly successful year for the Confederates in the East, but the South was still struggling. The Confederate forces in the West had failed to win a major battle, suffering defeat at places like Shiloh in Tennessee and across the Mississippi River. And as the war continued into 1863, the southern economy continued to deteriorate. Southern armies were suffering serious deficiencies of nearly all supplies as the Union blockade continued to be effective as stopping most international commerce with the Confederacy. Moreover, the prospect of Great Britain or France recognizing the Confederacy had been all but eliminated by the Emancipation Proclamation.

Given the unlikelihood of forcing the North's capitulation, the Confederacy's main hope for victory was to win some decisive victory or hope that Abraham Lincoln would lose his reelection bid in 1864, and that the new president would want to negotiate peace with the Confederacy. Understandably, this colored Confederate war strategy, and unquestionably Lee's.

After the Fredericksburg debacle and the "Mud March" fiasco that left a Union advance literally dead in its tracks, Lincoln fired Burnside and replaced him with "Fighting Joe" Hooker. Hooker had gotten his nickname from a clerical error in a newspaper's description of fighting, but the nickname stuck, and Lee would later playfully refer to him as F.J. Hooker. Hooker had stood out for his zealous fighting at Antietam, and the battle may very well have turned out differently if he hadn't been injured at the head of the I Corps. Now he was in command of a 100,000 man Army of the Potomac, and he devised a complex plan to cross the Rappahannock River with part of his force near Fredericksburg to pin down Lee while using the other bulk to turn Lee's left, which would allow his forces to reach the Confederate rear.

Hooker

Hooker's plan initially worked perfectly, with the division of his army surprising Lee. Lee was outnumbered two to one and now had to worry about threats on two fronts. Hooker was so confident that he informed his subordinates and Washington that Lee would be forced to flee.

As Longstreet alluded to in his memoirs, Lee was aggressive when he sensed an opportunity, and on May 1 he gambled that the Union forces north of Fredericksburg were merely a diversionary force that would not cause him trouble if he shifted the vast majority of his army to face the rest of Hooker's men near Chancellorsville. Thus, nearly 80% of Lee's army began marching west toward Chancellorsville in the early morning, leaving about 10,000 Confederates in Marye's Heights outside of Fredericksburg to defend against the 40,000 Union soldiers in their front. The rest of Lee's army, consisting of under 50,000 men, marched to the Zoan and Tabernacle churches along the Orange Turnpike and Orange Plank Road about two miles east of Chancellorsville. With that, the Confederates were outnumbered by 30,000 on their right and about 20,000 on their left.

While Lee's report makes clear that Hooker was in a strong defensive position, it was also in a position that would make troop movements much more difficult. On the other hand, the ground that the Union divisions were fighting over was high ground with enough openings to place and use artillery. However, instead of pushing his reserves forward, during the middle of the fighting Hooker ordered his advanced divisions to fall back to Chancellorsville, shocking the subordinates who were commanding men in the middle of the fray. Hooker was thus ceding the high ground around the roads and opting to dig in near the Wilderness instead, leaving some of the corps commanders beside themselves. George Meade complained, "My God, if we can't hold the top of the hill, we certainly can't hold the bottom of it!" Darius Couch also considered it the moment the battle was lost, writing, "Proceeding to the Chancellor House, I narrated my operations in front to Hooker, which were seemingly satisfactory, as he said: 'It is all right, Couch, I have got Lee just where I want him; he must fight me on my own ground.' The retrograde movement had prepared me for something of the kind, but to hear from his own lips that the advantages gained by the successful marches of his lieutenants were to culminate in fighting a defensive battle in that nest of thickets was too much, and I retired from his presence with the belief that my commanding general was a whipped man. The army was directed to intrench itself."

On the night of May 1, Lee still had to decide whether to pull his army back or attack Hooker. He was still hoping to destroy the entire portion of Hooker's army at Chancellorsville before Sedgwick and Reynolds began pushing back his sparse defensive line near Fredericksburg. Jackson agreed with him, and as the two met that night to discuss their options. Jackson biographer Robert Lewis Dabney described their meeting:

"When Friday night arrived, Generals Lee and Jackson met, at a spot where the road to the Catharine Iron Furnace turned southwestward from the plank-road, which was barely a mile in front of Hooker's works. Here, upon the brow of a gentle hill, grew a cluster of pine-trees, while the gound was carpeted with the clean, dry sedge and fallen leaves. They selected this spot, with their respective Staffs, to bivouac, while the army lay upon their weapons, a few yards before them, and prepared to sleep upon the ground, like their men. General Stuart had now joined them, and reported the results of his reconnoissances upon the south and west of Hooker's position. He had ascertained that the Federal commander had left a whole corps, under General Reynolds, at Ely's Ford, to guard his communications there, and that he had massed ninety thousand men around Chancellorsville, under his own eye, fortifying them upon the east, south and, southwest, as has been described. But upon the west and northwest his encampments were open, and their movements were watched by Stuart's pickets, who were secreted in the wilderness there. He had also ascertained, that almost all their cavalry had broken through the line of the Rapid Ann in one body, and had invaded the south, followed and watched by the brigade of W. H. Lee, evidently bent upon a grand raid against the Confederate communications. Generals Lee and Jackson now withdrew, and held an anxious consultation. That Hooker must be attacked, and that speedily, was clear to the judgments of both."

As Lee realized, however, "It was evident that a direct attack upon the enemy would be attended with great difficulty and loss, in view of the strength of his position and his superiority of numbers." Thanks to reports from Stuart's cavalry that Hooker's left was well-defended (thanks to Meade's march on River Road) and his right was "in the air" with an open flank, Lee decided "to endeavor to turn his right flank and gain his rear, leaving a force in front to hold him in check and conceal the movement." In other words, having already split his army in two in the face of a larger army, Lee now planned to split his army into three by having some of his command march around Hooker's right, defying all military convention. With that decision, the stage was set for two of the most dramatic days of the Civil War.

Having decided on the night of May 1 to try to turn Hooker's right flank, the Confederates went about getting a guide who could lead Jackson's command on the march. Charles C. Wellford, the man who owned the nearby Catherine Furnace, gave Jackson's mapmaker information about a road near Catherine Furnace that would take them to Brock Road and allow Jackson to march northwest toward Wilderness Tavern, placing them squarely in the flank and rear of Howard's XI Corps. The backwoods route was intended to hide the march from Union pickets, and the lack of Union cavalry to screen the Army of the Potomac made the stealthy march that much likelier to succeed.

As Jackson began marching his command that morning along a 12 mile route, Lee started digging in with Anderson's division and McLaws's division in Hooker's front along the Turnpike and the Plank Road. With Jackson's 28,000 men marching around Hooker's right, Lee now had less than 15,000 soldiers holding the line in front of Hooker's 70,000. Meanwhile, Hooker was also still digging in, and to bolster his numbers he ordered Reynolds to leave the Fredericksburg front and march to Chancellorsville to join the right flank. It was a circuitous march that had no hope of reaching Chancellorsville on May 2.

One of the great myths of Stonewall Jackson's legendary flank attack on May 2 is that it came as a complete surprise to the Army of the Potomac when the Confederates came bursting out of the woods on their flank. In fact, despite Stuart's cavalry screening the march in order to hide it to the best of their ability, there were several different times during the day that Union forces spotted the Confederate column and alerted their superiors. As Darius Couch explained:

"On the morning of May 2d our line had become strong enough to resist a front attack unless made in great force; the enemy had also been hard at work on his front, particularly that section of it between the Plank road and turnpike. Sedgwick, the previous night, had been ordered to send the First Corps (Reynolds's) to Chancellorsville. At 7 A. M. a sharp cannonade was opened on our left, followed by infantry demonstrations of no particular earnestness. Two hours later the enemy were observed moving a mile or so to the south and front of the center, and later the same column was reported to the commander of the Eleventh Corps by General Devens, whose division was on the extreme right flank. At 9:30 A. M. a circular directed to Generals Slocum and Howard called attention to this movement and to the weakness of their flanks."

News of Jackson's flank march reached Hooker within hours of its start, and Hooker guessed that it was either a retreat or a flanking march, so at 9:30 he warned XI Corps commander Oliver Howard, "We have good reason to suppose the enemy is moving to our right. Please advance your pickets for purposes of observation as far as may be safe in order to obtain timely information of their approach." Howard claimed later that morning that his corps was "taking measures to resist an attack from the west."

Around 3:00, Jackson and cavalry officer Fitzhugh Lee were able to scout the Union's lines from high ground near the Plank Road. Despite Howard having told Hooker that he was preparing for the possibility of an attack on his flank, Jackson found Howard's men idling around, completely unprepared for what was about to hit them. In addition to being unprepared, the XI Corps was composed of a bunch of raw recruits who had never seen battle, and those who had seen action performed poorly at Second Manassas. The very reason they were on the far right was because Hooker didn't intend to use them for major combat operations.

Around this time, Jackson sent his last two dispatches:

> "Near 3 p.m., May 2, 1863: General- The enemy has made a stand at Chancellor's, which is about two miles from Chancellorsville. I hope as soon as practicable to attack. I trust that an ever kind Providence will bless us with great success. Respectfully, T.J. JACKSON, Lieutenant General

> "Later—3:15 p.m. General- The leading division is up, and the next two appear to be well closed. T.J.J."

As Jackson's men reached the crossroads near Wilderness Tavern, the opening in the area allowed him to form battle lines that straddled the Orange Turnpike in the rear of the XI Corps. They would then be marching through thick underbrush that not only completely obscured them but also scratched them up and tore their clothes. Despite the inevitable noises made by 21,000 men moving forward through a forest, and the scurrying of various animals out of the forest, Howard's corps still remained unprepared, and many of them were mostly concerned with cooking their dinner.

The Stonewall Brigade was part of General Isaac Trimble's division and composed the rear of the marching column. The brigade was led by Brigadier General Elisha F. Paxton, who had assumed command on November 6, 1862. The men in file were unaware of their destination. Private John Casler remembered, "We could not imagine where we were going. We continued marching through the fields and woods until about three o'clock in the afternoon. The day was hot, and we marched fast the men throwing away their overcoats and blankets." He continued, "The other two divisions were in front of ours and we began to think Jackson was on one of his flank movements, when one of his couriers came back and told our General to hurry up his command, as General Jackson was waiting for it to form in line."[29] The Stonewall Brigade pushed on and reached the position of their first commander by late afternoon before the battle of the wilderness surrounding Chancellorsville commenced.

Sometime between 5:00-6:00 p.m., Jackson's men came hurtling out of the forest and fell upon Howard's hapless corps, many of whom had stacked unloaded rifles while sitting around campfires. Almost immediately, Jackson's attack rolled up Devens's division, and though Schurz's division tried to form an emergency defensive line in Jackson's front, they were quickly swept aside after finding themselves flanked on both sides. Dabney described the initial moments of the attack: "With a wild hurrah, the line of Rodes burst upon them from the woods, and the first volley decided their utter rout. The second line, commanded by Colston, unable to restrain their impetuosity, rushed forward at the shout, pressed upon the first, filling up their gaps, and firing over their heads, so that thenceforward the two were almost merged into one, and advanced together, a dense and impetuous mass. For three miles the Federalists were now swept back by a resistless charge. Even the works which confronted the west afforded them no protection; no sooner were they manned by the enemy, than the Confederates dashed upon them with the bayonet, and the defenders were either captured or again put to flight. The battle was but a continued onward march, with no other pause than that required for the rectification of the line, disordered by the density of the woods."

As Dabney's account suggests, the nature of the flank attack ensured that the Confederate officers began losing control of their commands almost immediately as they began rushing forward, but the XI Corps was even more out of control. Howard tried to valiantly rally his routed corps as they began fleeing in a panicked rout eastward, but he was no George H. Thomas and this was no Chickamauga. Most of his soldiers simply ran right past him until they reached Fairview, an open field near Hooker's headquarters at the Chancellor house. The vanguard of Jackson's attack, Robert Rodes's division, chased them the entire way until being brought to heel by the artillery posted there shortly after 7:00. Hooker tried to rally an emergency defensive line by pulling one of Sickles's III Corps divisions, who due to unusual sound acoustics had not heard any of the fighting despite the fact it was going on just 2.5 miles away from them, but it was the fading daylight that would ultimately blunt the Confederate attack.

The greatest resistance Jackson faced in his attack was the temptations that invited his men to stop their pursuit, including food, personal artifacts, guns, and other supplies. Jackson continued

---

[29] Casler, location, 1897.

to order his subordinates, "Press forward", and he tried to urge the soldiers to keep up what had now become a disorganized pursuit. The XI Corps had lost ¼ of its strength, 2,500 men (nearly half of whom had been captured), in an hour, while its general officers suffered a substantial number of casualties trying to rally their men. By the time the flank attack had petered out, Jackson's men were within sight of Hooker's headquarters at Chancellorsville, and Sickles's III Corps was now positioned between Jackson and the rest of Lee's force.

Lee had not been idle during Jackson's flank attack either, as explained by his nephew, cavalry officer Fitzhugh Lee, after the war: "During the flank march of his great lieutenant, Lee reminded the troops in his front of his position by frequent taps on different points of their lines, and when the sound of cannon gave notice of Jackson's attack, Lee ordered that Hooker's left be strongly pressed to prevent his sending re-enforcements to the point assailed."

Jackson's flank march permanently tarnished Oliver Howard's career and reputation, and he was well aware of it. In his post-campaign report, he took pains to try to explain what happened on the night of May 2:

"At about 6 p.m. I was at my headquarters, at Dowdall's Tavern, when the attack commenced. I sent my chief of staff to the front when firing was heard. General Schurz, who was with me, left at once to take command of his line. It was not three minutes before I followed. When I reached General Schurz's command, I saw that the enemy had enveloped my right, and that the First Division was giving way. I first tried to change the front of the deployed regiments. I next directed the artillery where to go; then formed a line by deploying some of the reserve regiments near the church. By this time the whole front on the north of the Plank road had given way. Colonel Buschbeck's brigade was faced about, and, lying on the other side of the rifle-pit embankment, held on with praiseworthy firmness. A part of General Schimmelfennig's and a part of General Krzyzanowski's brigades moved gradually back to the north of the Plank road and kept up their fire. At the center and near the Plank road there was a blind panic and great confusion. By the assistance of my staff and some other officers, one of whom was Colonel Dickinson, of General Hooker's staff, the rout was considerably checked, and all the artillery, except eight pieces, withdrawn. Some of the artillery was well served, and told effectively on the advancing enemy. Captain Dilger kept up a continuous fire until we reached General Betty's position.

Now as to the causes of this disaster to my corps:

1. Though constantly threatened and apprised of the moving of the enemy, yet the woods was so dense that he was able to mass a large force, whose exact whereabouts neither patrols, reconnaissances, nor scouts ascertained. He succeeded in forming a column opposite to and outflanking my right.

2. By the panic produced by the enemy's reverse fire, regiments and artillery were thrown suddenly upon those in position.

3. The absence of General Barlow's brigade, which I had previously located in reserve and en echelon with Colonel von Gilsa's, so as to cover his right flank. This was the only general reserve I had. My corps was very soon reorganized near Chancellorsville, and relieved General Meade's corps, on the left of the general line. Here it remained until Wednesday morning, when it resumed its position, as ordered, at the old camp."

Although the flank attack began to lose its steam as the sun went down, Jackson remained active all along his front, and in the process of conducting his own personal reconnaissance during the night, he positioned himself between the lines. Along with some of his staff, Jackson rode so closely to the Union line that some of the horses in his party were shot during a Union musket volley:

"He had now advanced a hundred yards beyond his line of battle, evidently supposing that, in accordance with his constant orders, a line of skirmishers had been sent to the front, immediately upon the recent cessation of the advance. He probably intended to proceed to the place where he supposed this line crossed the turnpike, to ascertain from them what they could learn concerning the enemy. He was attended only by a half dozen mounted orderlies, his signal officer, Captain Wilbourne, with one of his men, and his aide, Lieutenant Morrison, who had just returned to him. General A. P. Hill, with his staff also proceeded immediately after him, to the front of the line, accompanied by Captain Boswell of the Engineers, whom General Jackson had just detached to assist him. After the General and his escort had proceeded down the road a hundred yards, they were surprised by a volley of musketry from the right, which spread toward their front, until the bullets began to whistle among them, and struck several horses."

After that close call, Jackson, Hill, and the staffers started riding back toward their own lines, only to be confused for Union soldiers by their own men, soldiers of the 18th North Carolina:

"General Jackson was now aware of their proximity, and perceived that there was no picket or skirmisher between him and his enemies. He therefore, turned to ride hurriedly back to his own troops; and, to avoid the fire, which was, thus far, limited to the south side of the road, he turned into the woods upon the north side. It so happened that General Hill, with his escort, had been directed by the same motive almost to the same spot.

As the party approached within twenty paces of the Confederate troops, these, evidently mistaking them for cavalry, stooped, and delivered a deadly fire. So sudden and stunning was this volley, and so near at hand, that every horse which was not shot down, recoiled from it in panic, and turned to rush back, bearing their riders toward the approaching enemy. Several fell dead upon the spot, among them the amiable and courageous Boswell; and more were wounded. Among the latter was General Jackson. His right hand was penetrated by a ball, his left forearm lacerated by another, and the same limb broken a little below the shoulder by a third, which not only crushed the bone, but severed the main artery. His horse also dashed, panic-stricken, toward the enemy, carrying him beneath the boughs of a tree which inflicted severe blows, lacerated his face, and almost dragged him from the saddle. His bridle hand was now powerless, but seizing the reins with the right hand, notwithstanding its wound, he arrested his career, and brought the animal back toward his own lines.

General Jackson drew up his horse, and sat for an instant gazing toward his own men, as if in astonishment at their cruel mistake, and in doubt whether he should again venture to approach them."

After personally dressing Jackson's wounds, Hill briefly took command of the Second Corps, until he was himself wounded in the legs, leaving him unable to walk or ride a horse. Hill relinquished command to Rodes, who realized he was over his head and directed JEB Stuart himself to take temporary command of the Second Infantry Corps, a decision Lee seconded when news reached him.

A.P. Hill

Jackson had been nearly hit by Union gunfire, and after he was injured, a litter started trying to carry him to the rear while coming under Union artillery fire, causing even more troubles:

"The party was now met by a litter, which someone had sent from the rear; and the General was placed upon it, and borne along by two soldiers, and Lieutenants Smith and Morrison. As they were placing him upon it, the enemy fired a volley of canister-shot up the road, which passed over their heads. But they had proceeded only a few steps before the discharge was repeated, with a more accurate aim. One of the soldiers bearing the litter was struck down, severely wounded; and had not Major Leigh, who was walking beside it, broken his fall, the General would have been precipitated to the ground. He was placed again upon the earth; and the causeway was now swept by a hurricane of projectiles of every species, before which it seemed that no living thing could survive. The bearers of the litter, and all the attendants, excepting Major Leigh and the General's two aides, left him, and fled into the woods on either hand, to escape the fatal tempest; while the sufferer lay along the road, with his feet toward the foe, exposed to all its fury.

It was now that his three faithful attendants displayed a heroic fidelity, which deserves to go down with the immortal name of Jackson to future ages. Disdaining to save their lives by deserting their chief, they lay down beside him in the causeway, and sought to protect him as far as possible with their bodies. On one side was Major Leigh, and on the other Lieutenant Smith. Again and again was the earth around them torn with volleys of canister, while shells and minie balls flew hissing over them, and the stroke of the iron hail raised sparkling flashes from the flinty gravel of the roadway. General Jackson struggled violently to rise, as though to endeavor to leave the road; but Smith threw his arm over him, and with friendly force held him to the earth, saying: "Sir, you must lie still; it will cost you your life if you rise." He speedily acquiesced, and lay quiet; but none of the four hoped to escape alive. Yet, almost by miracle, they were unharmed; and, after a few moments, the Federalists, having cleared the road of all except this little party, ceased to fire along it, and directed their aim to another quarter."

After being painfully carried back behind the Confederate lines, Jackson had his left arm amputated. When Lee heard of Jackson's injuries, he sent his religious leader Chaplain Lacy to Stonewall with the message, "Give him my affectionate regards, and tell him to make haste and get well, and come back to me as soon as he can. He has lost his left arm, but I have lost my right arm."

In a chaotic turn of events, the Confederacy's famous cavalry chief, JEB Stuart, was now in charge of the bulk of Lee's infantry. Making matters even more difficult for a general who had been leading cavalry the entire war, he had to reorganize the corps, which had gotten intermingled and disorganized in the attack.

The Battle of Chancellorsville is best remembered for Stonewall Jackson's legendary flank attack on the night of May 2, but the battle would be decided on May 3. Despite the debacle suffered by the XI Corps, the Army of the Potomac still outnumbered Lee's army in the vicinity, and Jackson's corps (now commanded by Stuart) was still separated from the rest. Lee was determined to ensure Jackson's corps linked up with the rest of the army by attacking Sickles, whose III Corps stood between them along Hazel Grove.

In one of the most fateful decisions of the war, Lee's objective was actually obtained by Hooker's own orders. Early that morning, as the Confederates were preparing an attack despite being outnumbered by nearly 40,000 men, Hooker pulled the III Corps back from Hazel Grove to the Plank Road, covering his flanks and forming a horseshoe defensive line so that Sickles's corps would not be a salient in the line capable of being hit by both wings of the Confederate army around Chancellorsville. With that ground being ceded, Porter Alexander, who had been tasked by Stuart with conducting reconnaissance for placing artillery, was allowed to simply establish about 30 guns on the high ground at Hazel Grove. Alexander explained the consequences of Hooker's poor decision in his memoirs, "Altogether, I do not think there was a more brilliant thing done in the war than Stuart's extricating that command from the extremely critical position in which he found it."

As Hooker abandoned the high ground at Hazel Grove in favor of Fairview, Stuart's artillery began bombarding the Union positions from the high ground, not only forcing General Hooker's troops from Fairview but essentially decimating the Union lines while destroying Hooker's headquarters at Chancellor House. Of this turn of events, Stuart wrote, "As the sun lifted the mist that shrouded the field, it was discovered that the ridge on the extreme right was a fine position for concentrating artillery. I immediately ordered thirty pieces to that point, and, under the happy effects of the battalion system, it was done quickly. The effect of this fire upon the enemy's batteries was superb."

With Stuart's artillery now posted, the Confederates attacked all along the line at dawn, with Stuart's men advancing along the Plank Road from the west while Anderson and McLaws attacked up the Turnpike and Plank Road on the other side of Hooker's army. Stuart launched a savage attack with three divisions all advancing forward together, two of which were in support just a few hundred yards behind. Although many of them had exhausted themselves routing the XI Corps the night before, they were up to the challenge, as Stuart reported: "At early dawn, Trimble's division composed the second line and Rodes' division the third. The latter had his rations on the spot, and, as his men were entirely without food, was extremely anxious to issue. I was disposed to wait a short time for this purpose; but when, as preliminary to an attack, I ordered the right of the first line to swing around and come perpendicular to the road, the order was misunderstood for an order to attack, and that part of the line became engaged... In this hotly contested battle the enemy had strong works on each side of the road, those on the commanding ridge being heavily defended by artillery. The night also had given him time to mass his troops to meet this attack, but the desperate valor of Jackson's corps overcame every obstacle and drove the enemy to his new line of defense, which his engineers had constructed in his rear, ready for occupation, at the intersection of the Ely's Ford and United States Ford roads."

If Hooker had not regretted his decision to evacuate Hazel Grove earlier in the morning, he probably did around 9:00 a.m., when an artillery shell hit a pillar of the Chancellor house while he was standing near it. Hooker later noted that the shattered pillar struck him "violently... in an erect position from my head to my feet." It's long been speculated that Hooker suffered a concussion, but initially he refused to relinquish command to Couch or any of his staffers. Hooker's injury has long been cited as yet another reason why his generalship became more cautious after May 1.

Lee had managed to win every gamble he took from May 1-3, and he had masterfully defended his right while simultaneously striking at Hooker on his left, but the armies woke up on the morning of May 4 with the Army of the Potomac still heavily outnumbering the Army of Northern Virginia near Chancellorsville and near Salem Church just west of Fredericksburg. But throughout May 4, Hooker dug in, and during the next day, Hooker began the process of pulling his command back across the river, a delicate process that started with removing the artillery and clearing the roads so that the infantry would not get bottled up. In the early morning hours of May 6, the rest of the corps began crossing the river, with Meade's V Corps protecting the retreat on the south bank.

As a result, the Army of the Potomac was safely back on the other side of the river by May 6, greatly surprising Lee, who was still making plans to attack Hooker in hopes of destroying his command against the Rapidan. Incredibly, upon withdrawing back across the river and retreating, Hooker issued General Orders No. 49, which actually congratulated his army on their recent achievements.

The Chancellorsville campaign officially came to an end with Hooker's withdrawal on May 6, but the most important casualty of the campaign would not come until 4 days later.

After being wounded and carried behind the lines on the night of May 2, Stonewall Jackson had his arm amputated, after which he was transported to Thomas C. Chandler's plantation well behind the battle lines to convalesce. He seemed to be recovering, and his wife and newborn daughter joined him at the plantation, but his doctors were unaware Jackson was exhibiting common symptoms that indicated oncoming pneumonia. Jackson lay dying in the Chandler plantation outbuilding on Sunday, May 10, 1863 with his wife Anna at his side. He comforted his wife, telling her, "It is the Lord's Day...my wish is fulfilled. I always wanted to die on Sunday." Near the end, a delirious Jackson seemed to have his mind on war, blurting out, "Tell A. P. Hill to prepare for actions! Pass the infantry to the front! Tell Major Hawks..." His final words were "Let us cross over the river, and rest under the shade of the trees."

The loss of Jackson was a crushing one for the Confederacy and Lee's army. In his post-campaign report, Lee wrote of his fallen subordinate, "The movement by which the enemy's position was turned and the fortune of the day decided was conducted by the lamented Lieutenant-General Jackson, who, as has already been stated, was severely wounded near the close of the engagement on Saturday evening. I do not propose here to speak of the character of this illustrious man, since removed from the scene of his eminent usefulness by the hand of an inscrutable but all-wise Providence. I nevertheless desire to pay the tribute of my admiration to the matchless energy and skill that marked this last act of his life, forming, as it did, a worthy conclusion of that long series of splendid achievements which won for him the lasting love and gratitude of his country."

The Battle of Chancellorsville is widely remembered as Lee's greatest victory. Historian Robert Krick, who wrote a history of the campaign and titled his book *Lee's Greatest Victory*, notes, "Lee's Chancellorsville consisted of a pastiche of unbelievably risky gambits that led to a great triumph. Hooker's campaign, after the brilliant opening movements, degenerated into a tale of opportunities missed and troops underutilized." And from a tactical standpoint, there's no question that Chancellorsville was Lee's masterpiece. Every gamble paid off, every decision he made ended up being the right one, and he was assisted by skilled subordinates like Stuart and Jackson. He seamlessly switched between taking the offensive and skillfully defending on two separate fronts over the course of several days, and he ultimately forced an army more than twice the size of his to withdraw and abort the campaign.

However, as Longstreet noted in his memoirs, the context of the Chancellorsville campaign cannot be forgotten. Lee had gained a complete strategic and tactical victory, but it was more a result of Hooker becoming cautious. The casualties among the two sides were 17,000 Union soldiers killed, captured or wounded, with about 13,000 Confederates killed, captured, or wounded. In other words, Lee lost nearly 25% of his army, and though he inflicted 4,000 more casualties on Hooker's army, the Army of the Potomac lost about 15% of its manpower. The Confederates were undermanned and lacked the resources of the Union throughout the war, and while Lee had blunted the latest offensive by the Army of the Potomac, the campaign all but ended with the two armies in the same positions they had been in 10 days earlier. No matter how many times Lee won a battle like Chancellorsville, the Confederacy would still lose the war. As Longstreet would put it in his memoirs, "The battle as pitched and as an independent affair was brilliant, and if the war was for glory could be called successful, but, besides putting the cause upon the hazard of a die, it was crippling in resources and of future progress, while the wait of a few days would have given time for concentration and opportunities against Hooker more effective than we experienced with Burnside at Fredericksburg. This was one of the occasions where success was not a just criterion."

Naturally, an analysis of Chancellorsville far different today given the hindsight of knowing the Civil War's final result than it was in May 1863. At the time, Chancellorsville was one of the most stunning battles of the Civil War, and Lincoln was shook to the core, exclaiming after the battle, "My God! My God! What will the country say?" At the same time, the South's joy at hearing of the victory was completely dampened by the loss of Jackson, and Longstreet recalled that when he rejoined the army, "I found [Lee] in sadness, notwithstanding that he was contemplating his great achievement and brilliant victory of Chancellorsville, for he had met with great loss as well as great gains. The battle had cost heavily of his army, but his grief was over the severe wounding of his great lieutenant, General Thomas Jonathan Jackson, the head of the Second Corps of the Army of Northern Virginia; cut off, too, at a moment so much needed to finish his work in the battle so handsomely begun."

Ultimately, Chancellorsville's most decisive impact and legacy can be found in the many ways it shaped Lee's subsequent Pennsylvania Campaign. At the beginning of 1863, Lee felt the Confederate cause needed the kind of decisive victory and master stroke that could win the war with one grand battle. It's why Lee constantly felt compelled to attack an army twice his army's size multiple times at Chancellorsville, and his failure to knockout Hooker made him that much more anxious to win a crushing victory at Gettysburg.

Lee's impatience with the status quo after Chancellorsville also induced him to invade Pennsylvania in the first place. Knowing that victories on Virginia soil meant little to an enemy that could simply retreat, regroup, and then return with more men and more advanced equipment, Lee would next set his sights on a Northern invasion, aiming to turn Northern opinion against the war and against President Lincoln. With his men already half-starved from dwindling provisions, Lee intended to confiscate food, horses, and equipment as they pushed north, and he also hoped to influence Northern politicians into giving up their support of the war by penetrating into Harrisburg or even Philadelphia. Given the right circumstances, Lee's army might even be able to capture either Baltimore or Philadelphia and use the city as leverage in peace negotiations.

In the wake of Stonewall Jackson's death, Lee reorganized his army, creating three Corps out of the previous two, with A.P. Hill and Richard S. Ewell "replacing" Jackson. Hill had been a successful division commander, but he was constantly battling bouts of sickness that left him disabled, which would occur at Gettysburg. Ewell had distinguished himself during the Peninsula Campaign, but he suffered a serious injury during Second Manassas that historians often credit as making him more cautious in command upon his return. The Stonewall Brigade would henceforth be part of Ewell's corps.

General Ewell

Chapter 9: Gettysburg

In June 1863, Lee began his second invasion of the north, and with his men scattered across southeastern Pennsylvania, and with cavalry commander Stuart too far to the east to provide information, it is believed that one of the first notices Lee got about the Army of the Potomac's movements actually came from a spy named "Harrison", a man who apparently worked undercover for Longstreet but of whom little is known. Harrison reported that General Meade was now in command of the Union Army and was at that very moment marching north to meet Lee's army.

As a result, Lee was unaware of Meade's position when an advanced division of A.P. Hill's Corps marched toward Gettysburg on the morning of July 1. The battle began with John Buford's Union cavalry forces skirmishing against the advancing division of Henry Heth's just outside of town. Buford intentionally fought a delaying action that was meant to allow John Reynolds' I Corps to reach Gettysburg and engage the Confederates, which eventually set the stage for a general battle.

Buford

Reynolds, an effective general who had been considered for command of the entire army in place of Hooker and was considered by many the best general in the army, hurried his corps up to Gettysburg, including the Iron Brigade. Since Lee had invaded Pennsylvania, many believe that Reynolds, a native of the state, was even more active and aggressive than he might have otherwise been. In any event, Reynolds would be at the front positioning brigades that morning, and while he was directing part of the Iron Brigade, Reynolds fell from his horse, having been hit by a bullet behind the ear that killed him almost instantly. With his death, command of the I Corps fell upon Maj. Gen. Abner Doubleday, the Civil War veteran wrongly credited for inventing baseball.

Despite the death of the corps commander, the I Corps successfully managed to drive the Confederates in their sector back, highlighted by sharp fighting from the Iron Brigade. Around noon, the battle hit a lull, in part because Confederate division commander Henry Heth was under orders to avoid a general battle in the absence of the rest of the Army of Northern Virginia. At that point, however, the Union had gotten the better of the fighting, and the Confederate army was concentrating on the area, with more soldiers in Hill's corps in the immediate vicinity and Ewell's corps marching from the north toward the town.

As the Union's I Corps held the line, General Oliver O. Howard and his XI Corps came up on the right of the I Corps, eager to replace the stain the XI Corps had suffered at Chancellorsville thanks to Stonewall Jackson. As a general battle began to form northwest of town, news was making its way back to Meade several miles away that Reynolds had been killed, and that a battle was developing.

Meade had been drawing up a proposed defensive line several miles away from Gettysburg near Emmitsburg, Maryland, but when news of the morning's fighting reached him, Meade sent II Corps commander Winfield Scott Hancock ahead to take command in the field, putting him in temporary command of the "left wing" of the army consisting of the I, II, III and XI Corps. Meade also charged Hancock with determining whether to fight the general battle near Gettysburg or to pull back to the line Meade had been drawing up. Hancock would not be the senior officer on the field (Oliver Howard outranked him), so the fact that he was ordered to take command of the field demonstrates how much Meade trusted him.

As Hancock headed toward the fighting, and while the Army of the Potomac's I and XI Corps engaged in heavy fighting, they were eventually flanked from the north by Ewell's Confederate Corps, which was returning toward Gettysburg from its previous objective. For the XI Corps, it was certainly reminiscent of their retreat at Chancellorsville, and they began a disorderly retreat through the streets of the small town. Fighting broke out in various places throughout the town, while some Union soldiers hid in and around houses for the duration of the battle. Gettysburg's citizens also fled in the chaos and fighting.

After a disorderly retreat through the town itself, the Union men began to dig in on high ground to the southeast of the town. When Hancock met up with Howard, the two briefly argued over the leadership arrangement, until Howard finally acquiesced. Hancock told the XI Corps commander, "I think this the strongest position by nature upon which to fight a battle that I ever saw." When Howard agreed, Hancock replied, "Very well, sir, I select this as the battle-field."

As the Confederates sent the Union corps retreating, Lee arrived on the field and saw the importance of the defensive positions the Union men were taking up along Cemetery Hill and Culp's Hill. Late in the afternoon, Lee sent discretionary orders to Ewell that Cemetery Hill be taken "if practicable", but ultimately Ewell chose not to attempt the assault. Lee's order has been criticized because it left too much discretion to Ewell, leaving historians to speculate on how the more aggressive Stonewall Jackson would have acted on this order if he had lived to command this wing of Lee's army, and how differently the second day of battle would have proceeded with Confederate possession of Culp's Hill or Cemetery Hill. Discretionary orders were customary for General Lee because Jackson and Longstreet, his other principal subordinate, usually reacted to them aggressively and used their initiative to act quickly and forcefully. Ewell's decision not to attack, whether justified or not, may have ultimately cost the Confederates the battle. Edwin Coddington, widely considered the historian who wrote the greatest history of the battle, concluded, "Responsibility for the failure of the Confederates to make an all-out assault on Cemetery Hill on July 1 must rest with Lee. If Ewell had been a Jackson he might have been able to regroup his forces quickly enough to attack within an hour after the Yankees had started to retreat through the town. The likelihood of success decreased rapidly after that time unless Lee were willing to risk everything."

With so many men engaged and now taking refuge on the high ground, Meade, who was an engineer like Lee, abandoned his previous plan to draw up a defensive line around Emmittsburg a few miles to the south. After a council of war, the Army of the Potomac decided to defend at Gettysburg.

By the morning of July 2, Major General Meade had put in place what he thought to be the optimal battle strategy. Positioning his now massive Army of the Potomac in what would become known as the "fish hook", he'd established a line configuration that was much more compact and maneuverable than Lee's, which allowed Meade to shift his troops quickly from inactive parts of the line to those under attack without creating new points of vulnerability. Moreover, Meade's army was taking a defensive stance on the high ground anchored by Culp's Hill, Cemetery Hill, and Cemetery Ridge.

That morning, Lee decided to make strong attacks on both Union flanks while feinting in the middle, ordering Ewell's corps to attack Culp's Hill on the Union right while Longstreet's corps would attack on the Union left. Lee hoped to seize Cemetery Hill, which would give the Confederates the high ground to harass the Union supply lines and command the road to Washington, D.C. Lee also believed that the best way to do so would be to use Longstreet's corps to launch an attack up the Emmittsburg Road, which he figured would roll up the Union's left flank, presumed to be on Cemetery Hill. Lee was mistaken, due in part to the fact Stuart and his cavalry couldn't perform reconnaissance. In fact, the Union line extended farther south than Cemetery Hill, with the II Corps positioned on Cemetery Ridge and the III Corps nearly as far south as the base of Little Round Top and Round Top. Moreover, Ewell protested that this battle plan would demoralize his men, since they'd be forced to give up the ground they had captured the day before.

As it turned out, both attacks ordered by Lee would come too late. Though there was a controversy over when Lee ordered Longstreet's attack, Longstreet's march got tangled up and caused several hours of delay. Lost Cause advocates attacking Longstreet would later claim his attack was supposed to take place as early as possible, although no official Confederate orders gave a time for the attack. Lee gave the order for the attack around 11:00 a.m., and it is known that Longstreet was reluctant about making it; he still wanted to slide around the Union flank, interpose the Confederate army between Washington D.C. and the Army of the Potomac, and force Meade to attack them. Between Longstreet's delays and the mixup in the march that forced parts of his corps to double back and make a winding march, Longstreet's men weren't ready to attack until about 4:00 p.m.

The fighting on the Union left, which involved climactic fighting around Little Round Top, finally ended with the Northerners holding their ground that night. George Sykes, the commander of the V Corps, later described Day 2 in his official report, "Night closed the fight. The key of the battle-field was in our possession intact. Vincent, Weed, and Hazlett, chiefs lamented throughout the corps and army, sealed with their lives the spot intrusted to their keeping, and on which so much depended.... General Weed and Colonel Vincent, officers of rare promise, gave their lives to their country."

Meanwhile, Ewell's orders from Lee had been to launch a demonstration on the Union right flank during Longstreet's attack, which started at about 4:00 p.m. as well, and in support of the demonstration by Hill's corps in the center. For that reason, Ewell would not launch his general assault on Culp's Hill and Cemetery Hill until 7:00 p.m.

While the Army of the Potomac managed to desperately hold on the left, Ewell's attack against Culp's Hill on the other end of the field met with some success in pushing the Army of the Potomac back. However, the attack started so late in the day that nightfall made it impossible for the Confederates to capitalize on their success. Due to darkness, a Confederate brigade led by George H. Steuart was unaware that they were firmly beside the Army of the Potomac's right flank, which would have given them almost unlimited access to the Union army's rear and its supply lines and line of communication, just 600 yards away. Col. David Ireland and the 137th New York desperately fought to preserve the Union army's flank, much the same way Chamberlain and the 20th Maine had on the other side, and in the process the 137th lost a third of their men.

Steuart

Ewell's men would spend the night at the base of Culp's Hill and partially up the hill, in positions that had been evacuated by Union soldiers after Meade moved some of them to the left to deal with Longstreet's attack. It would fall upon the Confederates to pick up the attack the next morning.

That night, Meade held another council of war. Having been attacked on both flanks, Meade and his top officers correctly surmised that Lee would attempt an attack on the center of the line the next day. Moreover, captured Confederates and the fighting and intelligence of Day 2 let it be known that the only Confederate unit that had not yet seen action during the fighting was George Pickett's division of Longstreet's corps.

Members of the Stonewall Brigade had previously been sent into the woods on the left side of the line to force out Union sharpshooters. The brigade, therefore, did not participate in the initial attack up the hill. General Edward Johnson's division, of which the Stonewall Brigade was a part, was ordered to renew the attack on Culp's Hill on the morning of the third. Jackson's old brigade was forefront on the steep climb up the hill and struggled to find shelter behind rocks and other outcroppings. After climbing to a certain height, the timber had been decimated by shell and shot, leaving nowhere for the men to take cover. Simultaneous shooting from the Union forces exposed the Confederate attackers to what seemed like sheets of fire. Brigadier General James Walker at last order the brigade to withdraw, "'as it was a useless sacrifice of life to keep them longer under so galling a fire.'"[30] The Stonewall Brigade suffered 318 casualties at

Gettysburg, most coming during the charge up Culp's Hill.[31]

On the morning of July 3, the Confederate attack against Culp's Hill fizzled out, but by then Lee had already planned a massive attack on the Union center, combined with having Stuart's cavalry attack the Union army's lines in the rear. A successful attack would split the Army of the Potomac at the same time its communication and supply lines were severed by Stuart, which would make it possible to capture the entire army in detail.

There was just one problem with the plan, as Longstreet told Lee that morning: no 15,000 men who ever existed could successfully execute the attack. The charge required marching across an open field for about a mile, with the Union artillery holding high ground on all sides of the incoming Confederates. Longstreet ardently opposed the attack, but, already two days into the battle, Lee explained that because the Army of the Potomac was here on the field, he must strike at it. Longstreet later wrote that he said, "General Lee, I have been a soldier all my life. It is my opinion that no fifteen thousand men ever arrayed for battle can take that position."

Realizing the insanity of sending 15,000 men hurtling into all the Union artillery, Lee planned to use the Confederate artillery to try to knock out the Union artillery ahead of time. Although old friend William Pendleton was the artillery chief, the artillery cannonade would be supervised by Porter Alexander, Longstreet's chief artillerist, who would have to give the go-ahead to the charging infantry because they were falling under Longstreet's command.

As Longstreet had predicted, from the beginning the plan was an abject failure. As Stuart was in the process of being repulsed, just after 1:00 p.m. 150 Confederate guns began to fire from Seminary Ridge, hoping to incapacitate the Union center before launching an infantry attack, but they mostly overshot their mark. The artillery duel could be heard from dozens of miles away, and all the smoke led to Confederate artillery constantly overshooting their targets.

Eventually, Union artillery chief Henry Hunt cleverly figured that if the Union cannons stopped firing back, the Confederates might think they successfully knocked out the Union batteries. On top of that, the Union would be preserving its ammunition for the impending charge that everyone now knew was coming. When they stopped, Lee, Alexander, and others mistakenly concluded that they'd knocked out the Union artillery.

A short time later, the Confederates were prepared to step out for the charge that bears Pickett's name, even though he commanded only about a third of the force and was officially under Longstreet's direction. Today historians typically refer to the charge as the Pickett-Pettigrew-Trimble Assault or Longstreet's Assault to be more technically correct. Since A.P. Hill was sidelined with illness, Pettigrew's and Trimble's divisions were delegated to Longstreet's

[30] Smith, 81.
[31] Smith, 81. 2nd Virginia Infantry Regiment soldier, Wesley Culp died on the hill named after his family, who had at one time owned that section of land.

authority as well. To make matters worse, Hill's sickness resulted in organizational snafus. Without Hill to assign or lead troops, some of his battle-weary soldiers of the previous two days were tapped to make the charge while fresh soldiers in his corps stayed behind.

Thus, about 15,000 Confederates stepped out in sight and began their charge with an orderly march starting about a mile away, no doubt an inspiring sight to Hancock and the Union men directly across from the oncoming assault. Pickett launched his attack as ordered, but within five minutes the men came to the top of a low rise where his line came into full view of Union defenses. Though Pickett was seen galloping to the left to steady his men there, and one aide is said to remember him personally ordering the division to "double-quick" at the end of the advance, his exact whereabouts during the latter stages of the assault are unknown.

As the Confederate line advanced, Union cannon on Cemetery Ridge and Little Round Top began blasting away, with Confederate soldiers continuing to march forward. One Union soldier later wrote, "We could not help hitting them with every shot . . . a dozen men might be felled by one single bursting shell." By the time Longstreet's men reached Emmitsburg Road, Union artillery switched to firing grapeshot (tin cans filled with iron and lead balls), and as the Confederate troops continued to approach the Union center, Union troops positioned behind the wall cut down the oncoming Confederates, easily decimating both flanks. And while some of the men did mange to advance to the Union line and engage in hand-to-hand combat, it was of little consequence.

From almost the moment the Civil War ended, Gettysburg has been widely viewed as one of the decisive turning points of the Civil War. As renowned Civil War historian described Gettysburg, "It might be less of a victory than Mr. Lincoln had hoped for, but it was nevertheless a victory—and, because of that, it was no longer possible for the Confederacy to win the war. The North might still lose it, to be sure, if the soldiers or the people should lose heart, but outright defeat was no longer in the cards." While some still dispute that labeling, Lee's Army of Northern Virginia was never truly able to take the strategic offensive again for the duration of the war.

Naturally, if Gettysburg marked an important turning point in the Civil War, then to the defeated South it represented one of the last true opportunities the South had to win the war. After the South had lost the war, the importance of Gettysburg as one of the "high tide" marks of the Confederacy became apparent to everyone, making the battle all the more important in the years after it had been fought. Southern generals would argue for decades over who was most to blame, but perhaps none other than George Pickett himself put it best. When asked (certainly ad nauseam) why Pickett's Charge had failed, Pickett is said to have tersely replied, "I've always thought the Yankees had something to do with it."

Chapter 10: The End of the Stonewall Brigade

Gettysburg was the last time Lee's army would have the chance to be on the offensive during a campaign, as Grant's Overland Campaign ground both armies down across Virginia. By the early part of that campaign, the Stonewall Brigade would be all but spent as a fighting force.

Unlike McClellan, Burnside and Hooker before him, Grant's orders directed the Army of the Potomac to continue heading south. The Battle of the Wilderness had only been a beginning, not an ending. As Grant would famously telegraph Washington, D.C. a few days later, "I propose to fight it out on this line, if it takes all summer." If the Battle of the Wilderness had been a Confederate victory, that was an opinion lost on Grant's men when they learned the new marching orders.

With that, Grant began marching his army toward Spotsylvania Court House, the area he had hoped to reach before fighting Lee in a pitched battle. Things hadn't gone according to plan in the Wilderness, but Grant and Lee would have their battle at Spotsylvania soon enough.

When Grant ordered Meade on the night of May 7 to have the Army of the Potomac march to Spotsylvania Court House, he did so for several reasons. In addition to disengaging from Lee at the Wilderness and bring him out into the open, Grant hoped that swift marching might get his army inbetween Lee and Richmond, which would make the Confederates even more desperate.

Grant's route to Spotsylvania Court House had been opened by Phil Sheridan's cavalry in the days before, due to the fact that Grant had initially intended to march there before engaging in battle. Sheridan's cavalry had been holding important spots, including crossings of the Ny and Po Rivers, in anticipation of that movement, but when Hancock's left was turned by Longstreet's corps on May 6, the cavalry had been hurried back north. As a result, when Grant issued the orders to march toward Spotsylvania on May 7, it was once again incumbent on the Union cavalry to ride to those spots and hold them for the infantry advance.

The Confederates were not idle on May 7. The movements of the Union Army's logistics train had suggested to him that Grant was either moving east toward Fredericksburg or south toward Spotsylvania. Either way, Lee needed to hold the crossroads at Spotsylvania, so he gave orders to Richard Anderson's corps to occupy Spotsylvania Court House on May 8. Luckily for the Confederates, however, the desperate fighting of the 6th by that corps had sparked fires in the area of the fighting, and the putrid smells of the burning and death compelled Anderson and his soldiers to go ahead and march to Spotsylvania that night, rather than try to bivouac near the burning and dying. By 10:00 p.m., Anderson's corps was on the march toward Spotsylvania. Thus, if Grant was going to occupy Spotsylvania, he now needed to dislodge Anderson's corps or destroy it on May 8 before the rest of the Confederate army joined him.

As a result of Warren's inability to push Anderson's men at Laurel Hill, men from Ewell's corps, including the Stonewall Brigade, were able to slide into the line to the right of Anderson before John Sedgwick's VI Corps was in position on Warren's left. The two Union corps attempted a coordinated assault on the night of May 8, with Warren finally willing to put in all his men, but by then they were surprised to find Ewell's men in position and the assault was quickly and sharply repulsed.

By the end of the war, the Civil War had become a forerunner to the trench warfare of World War I, and if an army was given 24 hours to entrench, their position became practically unassailable. Thus, the Army of the Potomac's inability to clear Brock Road on May 8 allowed the Confederates to begin the process of digging in, a crucial advantage. Some generals who fought in the Civil War had come to believe that a well-entrenched defensive line could only be taken if there were 4 times as many attackers as defenders. John Gordon, who led a brigade in Early's corps, discussed the nature of the line as the Confederates dug in on the night of May 8:

"As the heads of the columns collided, the armies quickly spread into zigzag formation as each brigade, division, or corps struck its counterpart in the opposing lines. These haphazard collisions, however, rapidly developed a more orderly alignment and systematic battle, which culminated in that unparalleled struggle for the possession of a short line of Lee's breastworks. I say unparalleled, because the character of the fighting, its duration, and the individual heroism exhibited have no precedent, so far as my knowledge extends, in our Civil War, or in any other war.

During these preliminary and somewhat random engagements, General Lee, in order to secure the most advantageous locality offered by the peculiar topography of the country, had placed his battle line so that it should conform in large measure to the undulations of the field. Along the brow of these slopes earthworks were speedily constructed. On one portion of the line, which embraced what was afterward known as the 'Bloody Angle,' there was a long stretch of breastworks forming almost a complete semicircle. Its most advanced or outer salient was the point against which Hancock made his famous charge.

My command had been withdrawn from position in the regular line, and a role was assigned me which no officer could covet if he had the least conception of the responsibilities involved. I was ordered to take position in rear of that salient, and as nearly equidistant as practicable from every point of the wide and threatened semicircle, to watch every part of it, to move quickly, without waiting for orders, to the support of any point that might be assaulted, and to restore, if possible, any breach that might be made. We were reserves to no one command, but to all commands occupying that entire stretch of works. It will be seen that, with no possibility of knowing when or where General Grant would make his next effort to penetrate our lines, the task to be performed by my troops was not an easy one, and that the tension upon the brain and nerves of one upon whom rested the responsibility was not light nor conducive to sleep."

As the Confederates dug in, they were well aware that a salient was being created in the line at the Mule Shoe, which jutted out nearly a mile in front of the rest of their defensive line. Civil War armies always tried to avoid creating a salient in the line because it allowed the salient to be attacked in multiple directions. In this case, despite the fact the Mule Shoe was a salient, the Confederates dug in there to hold onto the nearest high ground in the area, hoping to prevent Union soldiers from occupying it and disrupting the rest of their line.

At the same time, the Army of the Potomac began digging in and erecting earthworks along their own lines, just as aware of their importance. With that, the two armies hunkered down into the kind of trench warfare that would've seemed foreign to the soldiers and generals in 1861. With sharpshooters among the lines, which were about half a mile away from each other, soldiers were afraid to even show their heads above their trenches for fear of being sniped.

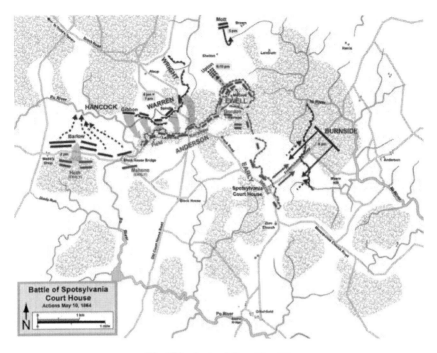

The "Bloody Angle" on May 10

On several occasions throughout the Overland Campaign, Grant ordered general attacks out of a sense that he could break Lee's army, and he had conceived of such an attack for May 10: "Accordingly in the morning, orders were issued for an attack in the afternoon on the centre by Warren's and Wright's corps, Hancock to command all the attacking force. Two of his divisions were brought to the north side of the Po. Gibbon was placed to the right of Warren, and Birney in his rear as a reserve. Barlow's division was left south of the stream, and Mott of the same corps was still to the left of Wright's corps. Burnside was ordered to reconnoitre his front in force, and, if an opportunity presented, to attack with vigor."

Grant's plan actually started to go haywire on the evening of May 9, when the Confederates noticed some of Hancock's II Corps shifting their position that night. This allowed Lee to counter the perceived threat by trying to outflank Hancock's corps with Early's corps, which led the Union high command to mistakenly assume that Early's men were being shifted to the Confederates' right flank.

Every attack made by the Army of the Potomac on May 10 was repulsed, and the lines had barely moved since the end of fighting on May 8, but Grant had reason for optimism. On May 11, he began plans to conduct another attack, this time with Hancock's entire II Corps instead of just 5,000 men. He also continued to believe that Lee's army was on the verge of being broken, partly the result of overestimating how many casualties he had inflicted on the Army of Northern Virginia and underestimating the Confederates.

After a couple of days in which Grant's incorrect assumptions had cost him chances for success, Lee made a terrible mistake on May 11 while reacting to movements by the Union army. Grant's plan for Hancock's assault required pulling his men out of the line and assembling them about a mile north of the Mule Shoe. By having Hancock attack the north face of the Mule Shoe while Wright advanced on the west face and Burnside advanced on the east face, the salient in the Confederate line would be as exposed as possible. Hancock's men would be advancing over open ground, while the part in the line they pulled out of was woody, which would keep Lee from fully understanding the movements and prevent the Confederates from launching a potentially devastating attack in the gap while Warren shifted to the left to replace Hancock's men.

Even worse, the movements of Hancock's corps and intelligence reports that Lee received convinced him that Grant was actually starting to retreat. Thinking this was the case, Lee intended to try to attack Grant's army while it was most vulnerable on the move, and since that would require improving the Army of Northern Virginia's mobility, he started withdrawing his artillery from around the salient for the purpose of having it prepared to advance more quickly.

As Hancock's men began moving to their staging ground at the Brown farm, thunderstorms provided a torrential downpour, making it that much harder to truly understand the purpose of the movement. That was of little comfort to Allegheny Johnson and his division, who were defending the salient in the line and watching Hancock's men marching north in their front even while their artillery was being withdrawn. Johnson pleaded with corps commander Richard Ewell to bring the guns back to his line, but by the time Ewell accepted the request and the orders reached the artillery units, it was 3:30 a.m. on the morning of May 12. Hancock's assault was scheduled to come crashing right into Allegheny Johnson's division just half an hour later.

As if Grant's attack hadn't already been aided by Lee pulling the artillery away from the salient, there was a dense fog over the battlefield when Hancock's men stepped off to begin their assault. Hancock's men would not have come into view until they were within 300 yards of the Confederate lines, and now they would be obscured by mist.

At 4:30 a.m. that morning, nobody could have believed what the salient would look like 24 hours later. Gettysburg hero Rufus Dawes, colonel of the 6th Wisconsin in the Iron Brigade, described the final approach to the salient and the nature of the entrenchments: "We stood perhaps one hundred feet from the enemy's line, and so long as we maintained a continual fire they remained hidden in their entrenchments. But if an attempt to advance was made, an order would be given and they would all rise up together and fire a volley upon us. They had constructed their works by digging an entrenchment about four feet deep, in which at intervals there were traverses to protect the flanks. This had the effect of making a row of cellars without drainage, and in them was several inches of mud and water. To protect their heads, they had placed in front logs which were laid upon blocks, and it was intended to put their muskets through the chinks under the head logs, but in the darkness this became impracticable and the head log proved a serious obstruction to their firing." Once again, the Iron Brigade would find themselves fighting around the same ground as the Stonewall Brigade.

As Hancock's men advanced, a rebel picket alerted the troops of the movement, and the men in the salient rose in unison to fire on their assailants. However, nearly all of the guns failed to fire as the caps and powder were soaked from the rain of the previous night. Northern troops poured over the breastworks around the salient and managed to encircle the Confederates within, and due to their faulty caps and no artillery present, the Stonewall Brigade fought with knives, bayonets, the butts of their guns, and their fists.[32]

Hancock's corps, nearly 15,000 strong, quickly overwhelmed the salient and almost immediately destroyed the initial defenders. As Hancock's men entered the Confederate trenches, Barlow's division fanned out to their left and flanked George Steuart's brigade facing Burnside's men on the eastern face of the Mule Shoe, capturing both Steuart and Allegheny Johnson. Meanwhile, David Birney's division advanced along the western part of the Mule Shoe until confronting the Stonewall Brigade, now commanded by James Walker.

Within half an hour, Hancock's corps had breached the Confederates' main line, capturing nearly 4,000 men and 20 guns, including their horses and ammunition. As the men kept advancing, Hancock had the captured Confederate guns turned around and began firing them down the Confederate lines, providing a devastating enfilade. Around this time, news of the initial success was making its way back to Grant's headquarters, and Theodore Lyman described the scene: "At a little after five o'clock, General Williams approached from the telegraph tent; a smile was on his face: Hancock had carried the first line! Thirty minutes after, another despatch: he had taken the main line with guns, prisoners and two generals! Great rejoicings now burst forth. Some of Grant's Staff were absurdly confident and were sure Lee was entirely beaten. My own experiences taught me a little more scepticism. Hancock presently sent to ask for a vigorous attack on his right, to cover and support his right flank. General Wright was accordingly ordered to attack with a part of the 6th Corps. As I stood there waiting, I heard someone say, 'Sir, this is General Johnson.' I turned round and there was the captured Major-General, walking slowly up. He was a strongly built man of a stern and rather bad face, and was dressed in a double-breasted blue-grey coat, high riding boots and a very bad felt hat. He was most horribly mortified at being taken, and kept coughing to hide his emotion. Generals Meade and Grant shook hands with him, and good General Williams bore him off to breakfast. His demeanor was dignified and proper.

---

[32] Smith, 88-91.

Not so a little creature, General Steuart, who insulted everybody who came near him, and was rewarded by being sent on foot to Fredericksburg, where there was plenty of mud and one stream up to his waist."

Horace Porter also recounted a rather tense exchange between Steuart and Hancock: "General George H. Steuart was also captured, but was not sent in to general headquarters on account of a scene which had been brought about by an unseemly exhibition of temper on his part. Hancock had known him in the old army, and in his usual frank way went up to him, greeted him kindly, and offered his hand. Steuart drew back, rejected the offer, and said rather haughtily, 'Under the present circumstances, I must decline to take your hand.' Hancock, who was somewhat nettled by this remark, replied, 'Under any other circumstances, general, I should not have offered it.'"

Burnside's men had attacked in concert with Hancock's and had greatly assisted in destroying the Confederate line on the eastern face of the Mule Shoe, but in the process his men had lost contact with the faster advancing II Corps. When Burnside informed Grant that his men had lost contact with Hancock's men, Grant responded, "Push the enemy with all your might; that's the way to connect."

Now, with a breach in the Confederate line nearly half a mile wide, both sides began quickly reacting by ordering more men to the fighting. For Grant, this meant that Wright's corps would support Hancock on the right, but because Grant had only planned for Wright to remain in a defensive posture during the initial assault, it required time for Wright's men to prepare for a similar kind of advance.

Meanwhile, Lee was so desperate that as he was ordering up reinforcements from John Gordon's division, he rode to the front of their marching column as though he was going to lead the charge himself. Fitzhugh Lee recalled the scene, writing, "On this occasion the general rode to the head of the column forming for the charge, took off his hat, and pointed to the captured line; but General John B. Gordon proposed to lead his own men, and no one in the army could do it better, for he was in dash and daring inferior to none. 'These are Virginians and Georgians who have never failed,' said Gordon. 'Go to the rear, General Lee.' And appealing to his men, he cried: 'Is it necessary for General Lee to lead this charge?' 'No, no,' they exclaimed; 'we will drive them back if General Lee will go to the rear.'

Gordon was unquestionably one of the toughest soldiers in the South. He had led a desperate flank attack at the Battle of the Wilderness on May 6, and he had been wounded several times at Antietam. But not even Gordon was ready for his division's initial contact with Hancock's corps:

"So rapidly and silently had the enemy moved inside of our works-- indeed, so much longer time had he been on the inside than the reports indicated--that before we had moved one half the distance to the salient the head of my column butted squarely against Hancock's line of battle. The men who had been placed in our front to give warning were against that battle line before they knew it. They were shot down or made prisoners. The sudden and unexpected blaze from Hancock's rifles made the dark woodland strangely lurid. General Johnson, who rode immediately at my side, was shot from his horse, severely but not, as I supposed, fatally wounded in the head. His brigade was thrown inevitably into great confusion, but did not break to the rear. As quickly as possible, I had the next ranking officer in that brigade notified of General Johnson's fall and directed him at once to assume command. He proved equal to the emergency. With great coolness and courage he promptly executed my orders. The Federals were still advancing, and every movement of the North Carolina brigade had to be made under heavy fire. The officer in charge was directed to hastily withdraw his brigade a short distance, to change front so as to face Hancock's lines, and to deploy his whole force in close order as skirmishers, so as to stretch, if possible, across the entire front of Hancock. This done, he was ordered to charge with his line of skirmishers the solid battle lines before him. His looks indicated some amazement at the purpose to make an attack which appeared so utterly hopeless, and which would have been the very essence of rashness but for the extremity of the situation. He was, however, full of the fire of battle and too good a soldier not to yield prompt and cheerful obedience. That order was given in the hope and belief that in the fog and mists which concealed our numbers the sheer audacity of the movement would confuse and check the Union advance long enough for me to change front and form line of battle with the other brigades. The result was not disappointing except in the fact that Johnson's brigade, even when so deployed, was still too short to reach across Hancock's entire front. This fact was soon developed: not by sight, but by the direction from which the Union bullets began to come."

As Gordon's account indicated, the fog and damp conditions made musket volleys and firing far more ineffective than they otherwise would have usually been. Moreover, the nature of the Confederate lines, which were composed of trenches that were upwards of 4 feet deep in some positions, made it all but impossible for Hancock's corps to reform their battle lines once they had stormed the Confederates' positions. With men getting mixed up in the chaos, it became impossible for officers to control their commands, and the fighting around the breached salient began to devolve into hand-to-hand fighting.

As Hancock was proudly boasting, "I have used up Johnson and am going into Early", Gordon's division came countercharging into the breach and checked Hancock's progress with a series of desperate attacks. As they began to push back Hancock's now-exhausted attackers on the eastern portion of the Mule Shoe, division commander Robert Rodes was reestablishing the Confederate line on the western part of the Mule Shoe.

The Confederates had just desperately stopped Hancock's momentum, but the worst was yet to come. By the time the Confederates had fought off Hancock, Wright's entire corps was ready to press forward around 6:30 a.m., and Grant had also ordered Warren's corps to attack the Confederates on their left and pin them down. By now, the steady rain that was still coming down had combined with the mud and the blood of the fighting soldiers to produce a nauseating stream in the trenches near the salient that one soldier recalled being half-way up to his knees. It was only about to get worse.

Around 6:30 a.m., Wright's corps had been assembled in a similar manner to Upton's assault, and they rushed forward into the salient even while some of Hancock's men were streaming to the rear. G. Norton Galloway, a member of the 95th Pennsylvania in Wright's corps, described the scene:

"Under cover of the smoke-laden rain the enemy was pushing large bodies of troops forward, determined at all hazards to regain the lost ground. Could we hold on until the remainder of our brigade should come to our assistance? Regardless of the heavy volleys of the enemy that were thinning our ranks, we stuck to the position and returned the fire until the 5th Maine and the 121st New York of our brigade came to our support, while the 96th Pennsylvania went in on our right ; thus reenforced, we redoubled our exertions. The smoke, which was dense at first, was intensified by each discharge of artillery to such an extent that the accuracy of our aim became very uncertain, but nevertheless we kept up the fire in the supposed direction of the enemy. Meanwhile they were crawling forward under cover of the smoke, until, reaching a certain point, and raising their usual yell, they charged gallantly up to the very muzzles of our pieces and reoccupied the Angle.

Upon reaching the breastwork, the Confederates for a few moments had the advantage of us, and made good use of their rifles. Our men went down by the score; all the artillery horses were down ; the gallant Upton was the only mounted officer in sight. Hat in hand, he bravely cheered his men, and begged them to 'hold this point.' All of his staff had been either killed, wounded, or dismounted.

At this moment, and while the open ground in rear of the Confederate works was choked with troops, a section of Battery C, 5th United States Artillery, under Lieutenant Richard Metcalf, was brought into action and increased the carnage by opening at short range with double charges of canister. This staggered the apparently exultant enemy. In the maze of the moment these guns were run up by hand close to the famous Angle, and fired again and again, and they were only abandoned when all the drivers and cannoneers had fallen. The battle was now at white heat.

The rain continued to fall, and clouds of smoke hung over the scene. Like leeches we stuck to the work, determined by our fire to keep the enemy from rising up. Captain John D. Fish, of Upton's staff, who had until this time performed valuable service in conveying ammunition to the gunners, fell, pierced by a bullet. This brave officer seemed to court death as he rode back and forth between the caissons and cannoneers with stands of canister under his 'gum' coat. 'Give it to them , boys! I'll bring you the canister,' said he; and as he turned to cheer the gunners, he fell from his horse, mortally wounded. In a few moments the two brass pieces of the 5th Artillery, cut and hacked by the bullets of both antagonists, lay unworked with their muzzles projecting over the enemy's works, and their wheels half sunk in the mud. Between the lines and near at hand lay the horses of these guns, completely riddled. The dead and wounded were torn to pieces by the canister as it swept the ground where they had fallen."

Earthworks near the Bloody Angle

With Wright's VI Corps crashing into the line, the Confederates were forced to quickly bring in more reinforcements, beginning with William Mahone's division. Mahone had been near the extreme left the previous day while Heth's division was attacking the Union's right flank, and now he was forced to quickly countermarch two of his brigades from the extreme left to the Mule Shoe. By 9:30 a.m., all of the VI Corps had been committed and were desperately fighting to hold on as more Confederates streamed to the breach.

As Lee kept pulling men from his left to reinforce the Mule Shoe, a stalemate developed in which neither side could fully dislodge the other. For Lee, this meant that Union artillery positions made his current defensive line precarious, while Grant was still holding out hope of achieving a decisive breakthrough that would cut Lee's army in two, separating Ewell and Early from Anderson. As a result, both commanders kept ordering more and more men forward into the salient.

By the mid-afternoon, the Union and Confederate soldiers had been fighting at the salient for over 10 hours. Galloway discussed the nature of the fighting at the Bloody Angle during this time:

"The great difficulty was in the narrow limits of the Angle, around which we were fighting, which precluded the possibility of getting more than a limited number into action at once. At one time our ranks were crowded in some parts four deep by reenforcements. Major Henry P. Truefitt, commanding the 119th Pennsylvania, was killed, and Captain Charles P. Warner, who succeeded him, was shot dead. Later in the day Major William Ellis, of the 49th New York, who had excited our admiration, was shot through the arm and body with a ramrod during one of the several attempts to get the men to cross the works and drive off the enemy. Our losses were frightful. What remained of many different regiments that had come to our support had concentrated at this point and planted their tattered colors upon a slight rise of ground close to the Angle, where they staid during the latter part of the day.

To keep up the supply of ammunition pack mules were brought into use, each animal carrying three thousand rounds. The boxes were dropped close behind the troops engaged, where they were quickly opened by the officers or file-closers, who served the ammunition to the men. The writer fired four hundred rounds of ammunition, and many others as many or more. In this manner a continuous and rapid fire was maintained, to which for a while the enemy replied with vigor.

Finding that we were not to be driven back, the Confederates began to use more discretion, exposing themselves but little, using the loop-holes in their works to fire through, and at times placing the muzzles of their rifles on the top logs, seizing the trigger and small of the stock, and elevating the breech with one hand sufficiently to reach us."

However, while more and more men packed into the tight lines, Lee was busy creating a new defensive line south of the Mule Shoe that would prevent him from having to defend a salient. All throughout the afternoon Confederate engineers began shuffling men south of the fighting and digging in, so that there would be a new set of entrenchments for the Confederates to use once the new line was established.

When dawn broke on the 13th, the Bloody Angle produced a sight unlike anything the battle hardened soldiers had seen before. Theodore Lyman recounted injured men being pulled out from under multiple corpses, and seeing one corpse that looked like it had been shot 80 times. Dawes, who had fought at Antietam and Gettysburg, was so horrified by the Bloody Angle that he ordered his men to pull out so they wouldn't have to sleep near the spot, writing, "In the morning the rebel works presented an awful spectacle. The cellars were crowded with dead and wounded, lying in some cases upon each other and in several inches of mud and water. I saw the body of a rebel soldier sitting in the corner of one of these cellars in a position of apparent ease, with the head entirely gone, and the flesh burned from the bones of the neck and shoulders. This was doubtless caused by the explosion of a shell from some small Cohorn mortars within our lines."

Grants aide, Horace Porter, was astounded by what he saw: "The appalling sight presented was harrowing in the extreme. Our own killed were scattered over a large space near the "angle," while in front of the captured breastworks the enemy's dead, vastly more numerous than our own, were piled upon each other in some places four layers deep, exhibiting every ghastly phase of mutilation. Below the mass of fast-decaying corpses, the convulsive twitching of limbs and the writhing of bodies showed that there were wounded men still alive and struggling to extricate themselves from the horrid entombment. Every relief possible was afforded, but in too many cases it came too late. The place was well named the 'Bloody Angle.'"

Galloway noted one morbid way that the Union soldiers still holding the salient went about burying the dead: "Hundreds of Confederates, dead or dying, lay piled over one another in those pits. The fallen lay three or four feet deep in some places, and, with but few exceptions, they were shot in and about the head. Arms, accouterments, ammunition, cannon, shot and shell, and broken foliage were strewn about. With much labor a detail of Union soldiers buried the dead by simply turning the captured breastworks upon them. Thus had these unfortunate victims unwittingly dug their own graves. The trenches were nearly full of muddy water. It was the most horrible sight I had ever witnessed."

Lee's army had barely escaped disaster on the 12th, leaving Grant anxious to continue offensive operations, but he was also well aware that an attack against the newly entrenched line would be suicidal. Grant was finally convinced of the hopelessness of striking a decisive blow at Spotsylvania Court House, noting in his memoirs, "I immediately gave orders for a movement by the left flank, on towards Richmond, to commence on the night of the 19th. I also asked Halleck to secure the cooperation of the navy in changing our base of supplies from Fredericksburg to Port Royal, on the Rappahannock."

The Battle of Spotsylvania Courthouse marked the end of the Stonewall Brigade for all practical purposes. After being pushed back in the Wilderness, General Grant surprised everyone by not retreating. He evacuated his wounded and pushed eastward, attempting yet another flanking tactic. Lee understood what Grant was planning and raced to a crossroads called Spotsylvania Courthouse. The Confederates beat Grant's troops to the position and began entrenching on the high ground. The defensive line was formed in such a manner that a salient formed in the center of the line; referred to by the men as the "Mule Shoe."[33] Artillery pieces were positioned in the salient along with the infantrymen of the Stonewall Brigade. On May 10, a slight but forceful attack on the salient was attempted by the Union. They had initial success,

---

[33] Cutrer, Lecture, April 20, 2011.

but were repelled in short order by the Stonewall Brigade. The following day, Lee feared another flanking maneuver by Grant and ordered that the artillery guns be pulled back from the salient to facilitate a swift withdrawal if necessary. That night the Stonewall Brigade remained alert in the rain; anticipating a Yankee attack. The following morning (12th) at dusk, General Winfield Scott Hancock and his 20,000 man corps began their assault on the Mule Shoe. A Rebel picket alerted the troops of the movement and the men in the salient rose in unison to fire on their assailants. Nearly all of the guns failed to fire as the caps and powder were soaked from the rain of the previous night. With little to no resistance, Northern troops poured over the breastworks around the salient and managed to encircle the Confederates within. With faulty caps and no artillery present, the Stonewall Brigade fought with knife, bayonet, gun butt, and fist. Those who were able, fled; the remainder were killed.[34]

By May 14, 1864, there were less than 200 members of the Stonewall Brigade still in action. These men and survivors from other Virginia brigades were combined to form one small brigade, which was commanded by William Terry as the 4th Virginia.[35] Terry's Brigade, as it became known simply as a means of designation, fought in various encounters for the remainder of the war, and the men of the former 1st Brigade, Virginia Volunteers, continued to refer to themselves as members of the Stonewall Brigade.

After General Grant successfully completed the Union's siege on Petersburg and the ensuing capture of Richmond, the Confederate capital, the rebellion was pragmatically at an end. April 9, 1865 was the day on which General Robert E. Lee surrendered the Army of Northern Virginia to General Ulysses S. Grant at Appomattox Courthouse, Virginia. Grant offered generous terms wherein he allowed the surrendering troops to maintain possession of their personal arms and horses in exchange for each man signing an oath of loyalty to the United States. The capitulation by Lee was handled quite amicably as Grant ordered his troops to provide rations to the defeated rebel soldiers and forbade cheering or any type of instigation from his men.

The formal surrender ceremony, during which the defeated troops stacked their arms, took place on April 12, exactly four years to the day the first shots were fired at Fort Sumter. Colonel Joshua Lawrence Chamberlain of the 20th Maine, who so valiantly defended Little Round Top at Gettysburg on July 2, 1863, was in command of the Union troops assembled in formation to observe and accept the stacking of arms. In deference to the officers of Lee's army, Chamberlain lowered his sword in an officer's salute as each ranking member of his former enemy passed by. Leading the parade of surrender were the surviving members of the Stonewall Brigade.

Appendix A: Original Regiments and Companies of the Stonewall Brigade

2nd Virginia Infantry Regiment:

---

[34] Smith, 88-91.
[35] Smith, 91.

(A) Company- Jefferson Guards, Jefferson, County.

(B) Company- Hamtramck Guards, Shepadstown.

(C) Company- Nelson Rifles, Millwood.

(D) Company- Berkeley Border Guards, Berkeley.

(E) Company- Hedgesville Blues, Martinsburg.

(F) Company- Winchester Riflemen, Winchester.

(G) Company- Botts Greys, Charlestown.

(H) Company- Letcher Riflemen, Duffields community.

(I) Company- Clarke Rifles, Berryville.

(K) Company- Floyd Guards, Harpers Ferry.

4th Virginia Infantry Regiment:

(A) Company- Wythe Grays, Wytheville.

(B) Company- Fort Lewis Volunteers, Big Spring region.

(C) Company- Pulaski Guards, Pulaski, County.

(D) Company- Smythe Blues, Marion.

(E) Company- Montgomery Highlanders, Blacksburg.

(F) Company- Grayson Daredevils, Elk Creek.

(G) Company- Montgomery Fencibles, Montgomery County.

(H) Company- Rockbridge Grays, Buffalo Forge and Lexington.

(I) Company- Liberty Hall Volunteers, Lexington.

(K) Company- Montgomery Mountain Boys, Montgomery County.

5th Virginia Infantry Regiment:

(A) Company- Marion Rifles, Winchester.

(B) Company- Rockbridge Rifles, Rockbridge County.

(C) Company- Mountain Guard, Staunton.

(D) Company- Southern Guard, Staunton.

(E) Company- Augusta Grays, Greenville community.

(F) Company- West View Infantry, Augusta County.

(G) Company- Staunton Rifles, Staunton.

(H) Company- Augusta Rifles, Augusta County.

(I) Company- Ready Rifles, Sangerville community.

(K) Company- Continental Morgan Guards, Frederick County.

(L) Company- West Augusta Guards, Staunton.

27th Virginia Infantry Regiment:

(A) Company- Allegheny Light Infantry, Covington.

(B) Company- Virginia Hiberians, Alleghany County.

(C) Company- Allegheny Rifles, Clifton Forge.

(D) Company- Monroe Guards, Monroe County.

(E) Company- Greenbrier Rifles, Lewisburg.

(F) Company- Greenbrier Sharpshooters, Greenbrier County.

(G) Company- Shriver Grays, Wheeling.

(H) Company- Rockbridge Rifles (this company was initially attached to

B Company of the 5th regiment).

33rd Virginia Infantry Regiment:

(A) Company- Potomac Guards, Springfield, Hampshire County.[36]

---

[36] This was the company to which Private John O. Casler belonged.

(B) Company- Tom's Brook Guard, Tom's Brook, Shenandoah County.

(C) Company- Tenth Legion Minute Men, Woodstock, Shenandoah County.

(D) Company- Mountain Rangers, Winchester, Frederick County.

(E) Company- Emerald Guard, New Market, Shenandoah County.

(F) Company- Independent (Hardy) Grays, Moorefield, Hardy County.

(G) Company- Mount Jackson Rifles, Mount Jackson region, Shenandoah, County.

(H) Company- Page Grays, Luray, Page County.

(I) Company- Rockingham Confederates, Harrisonburg, Rockingham County.

(K) Company- Shenandoah Sharpshooters, Shenandoah County.

Appendix B: Brigade Commanders

Brigadier General Thomas J. Jackson: April 27- October 28, 1861.

Brigadier General Richard B. Garnett: November 14, 1861- March 25, 1862.

Brigadier General Charles S. Winder: March 25- August 9, 1862.

Colonel William Baylor: August 9-30, 1862.

Lieutenant Colonel Andrew J. Grigsby: August 30- November 6, 1862.

Brigadier General Elisha F. Paxton: November 6, 1862- May 3, 1863.

Brigadier General James A. Walker: May 14, 1863- May 12, 1864.

Brigadier General William Terry: May 14, 1864 assumed command of surviving members of the Stonewall Brigade until the surrender at Appomattox Courthouse, April 9, 1865.

Online Resources

Other Civil War titles by Charles River Editors

Other books about 19th century American history by Charles
River Editors

Other books about Stonewall Jackson and the Stonewall Brigade
on Amazon

Bibliography

Barry, Joseph. *The Strange Story of Harpers Ferry: With Legends of the Surrounding Country.*

Martinsburg, W. VA: Thompson Brothers, 1903.

Casler, John O. *Four Years in the Stonewall Brigade.* 2nd ed., 1906. Endeavour Press, 2016.

Kindle.

Cutrer, Thomas. Lectures. Glendale, AZ, February-May, 2011.

Freeman, Douglas S. *Lee's Lieutenants: A Study in Command.* 3 vols. New York: 1943-44.

Foner, Eric. *Give Me Liberty! An American History.* Vol. 1, 2nd ed. New York: W.W. Norton

and Company, 2009.

Imboden, John B. "Stonewall Jackson in the Shenandoah," in *Battles and Leaders of the Civil*

War. Edited by Clarence C. Buel and Robert U. Johnson. 4 vols. New York: 1888.

Jackson, Mary Anna. *Memoirs of "Stonewall" Jackson.* Louisville: Prentice Press, 1895.

McPherson, James. *Antietam: The Battle That Changed the Course of the Civil War.* New York:

Oxford University Press, 2002.

_____. *Battle Cry of Freedom: The Civil War Era.* New York: Oxford University

Press, 1998.

Smith, Steven M. and Patrick Hook. *The Stonewall Brigade in the Civil War.* Minneapolis:

Zenith Press, 2008.

United States War Department. *The War of the Rebellion: A Compilation of the Official Records*

Of the Union and Confederate Armies, 128 vols. Washington, D.C.: Government

Printing Office, 1888.

Made in the USA
Middletown, DE
17 December 2018